# A MATTER OF LAW

# A MATTER OF LAW

*A Memoir of Struggle in the
Cause of Equal Rights*

**Robert L. Carter**

**THE NEW PRESS**

NEW YORK
LONDON

Requests for permission to reproduce selections from this book
should be mailed to: Permissions Department, The New Press,
38 Greene Street, New York, NY 10013

Published in the United States by The New Press, New York, 2005
Distributed by W. W. Norton & Company, Inc., New York

Library of Congress Cataloging-in-Publication Data
Carter, Robert L., 1917–
A matter of law : a memoir of struggle in the cause of equal rights /
Robert L. Carter.
p. cm.
Includes index.
ISBN 1-56584-830-6 (hardcover)
1. Carter, Robert L., 1917–  2. African American lawyers—Biography.
3. African American civil rights workers—Biography.  4. African Americans—
Civil rights—History—20th century.  5. Segregation—Law and legislation—
United States—History—20th century.  6. Race discrimination—Law and
legislation—United States—History—20th century.  I. Title.
KF373.C378A3    2005
340'.092—dc22            2004059298
[B]

The New Press was established in 1990 as a not-for-profit alternative to the large,
commercial publishing houses currently dominating the book publishing industry.
The New Press operates in the public interest rather than for private gain, and is
committed to publishing, in innovative ways, works of educational, cultural, and
community value that are often deemed insufficiently profitable.

www.thenewpress.com

Composition by dix!

Printed in the United States of America

2   4   6   8   10   9   7   5   3   1

# Contents

# *Acknowledgments*

Since I have written my memoir so late in life, many of the people who urged me to write have gone on, but probably are as, if not more, responsible than those now living for my actually taking the essential first step in exerting time and effort to produce this record of the salient events of my personal and professional life. These include my wife, Gloria; my good friend and traveling companion, Rose Reiter, with whom I saw most of Europe and much of Asia, India, China, and Japan; and Franklin Williams, the director of Columbia University's Urban Center in the late 1960s and the closest and best male friend I had of my own age, whom I disappointed for not writing this when I was a fellow at Columbia under a grant supplied by him. I was not ready then, and only found whatever energy or desire needed to start writing my story in July 2002, at the age of eighty-five.

Fortunately, many who gave me sustenance and encouragement will see the finished product. Among those to whom I am deeply indebted is Derrick Bell, who tried to stir up the interest of several publishers. There were a number of other friends who tried to help, but the needed spark was supplied by Patricia Sullivan and Waldo Martin. On reading the manuscript I had been peddling, they saw possibilities and helped me recast the original document into a piece better designed to produce a publisher's interest and which The New Press found sufficient to take me on as one of its authors. Without Pat and Waldo's interest and knowledge, the original manuscript would still be gathering dust in my files. Marc Favreau, my editor, has been especially helpful and generous. Indeed, this has been such a warm and enjoyable experience I wish I had started years ago, and perhaps several books might have been produced.

I am particularly indebted to the John Kluge Fellowship at the Library of Congress, and to Dr. James H. Billington, the Librarian of Congress, and Prosser Gifford, Director of Scholarly Programs, who were responsible for my receiving it. The fellowship enabled me to study the Library of Congress's NAACP collection, the contents of which inform much of the memoir. For me the Library was a wonderful place for research, writing and contemplation. My work at the Library was aided by the invaluable assistance of two visiting scholars, Phyllis McClure and Larissa Smith. They were fun to work with and we forged a bond of affection in the process. I would also like to thank David Foster for his tireless work on this project.

Finally, I am also indebted to the W.E.B. Du Bois Institute of Harvard University, the Harvard University Law School and its dean, Robert C. Clark, and Henry Louis Gates Jr., W.E.B. Du Bois Professor of Humanities and noted author, for a grant enabling me to spend time in residence at the Du Bois Institute working on this manuscript. I am also grateful to Charles J. Ogletree Jr. for awarding me a grant as the first Charles Hamilton Houston fellow, pursuant to which this manuscript was completed in August 2004.

A great many people had faith in me, and I hope they will feel the finished product for which they provided the means of production vindicates their faith.

# Foreword

In the late summer of 1953 I had the honor and pleasure of serving on Thurgood Marshall's nonlegal research staff of the NAACP Legal Defense Fund. Our duty was to assist in answering the questions raised by the United States Supreme Court over the intent of the framers of the Fourteenth Amendment regarding segregation in the public schools. The group worked hard to find the answers. If we did not provide direct and satisfactory answers to the Court's query, we did succeed, I believe, in providing aid and comfort to Marshall and his colleagues about the history of segregated public schools and of the Reconstruction period in general. It was gratifying to notice, as the weeks and months passed, the ease and erudition with which these civil rights lawyers handled the legal and social history of the Reconstruction era.

Among the lawyers assisting Marshall was a man so

youthful in appearance and so unprepossessing in manner that I assumed he was a student aide or intern of some sort. Then, at the initial conference where the lawyers met with the nonlegal staff in September of 1953, this same young man, Robert L. Carter, spoke up with such assurance and confidence that I was certain that he was not the messenger-aide I had previously assumed him to be. He was, indeed, a seasoned, well-informed, and trusted colleague of Thurgood Marshall. As the weeks passed and as I regularly noted his mastery of the legal intricacies of the Reconstruction years and beyond, my admiration and respect for him grew. He was by that time my idea of a lawyer's lawyer, an authority on the legal history of the Reconstruction years and beyond, and a valued and trusted senior member of the Legal Defense Fund staff.

In the autumn of 1953, as I made my weekly journey from Washington to New York to work in Marshall's office, I got to know Carter much better, and with every passing week I came to admire and respect him more. I especially cheered him when he successfully fought the state of Alabama's determined efforts to shut down the NAACP's activities there. This was the beginning of a series of actions on the part of states in the South to terminate the activities of the premier civil rights organization. It was Carter, more than anyone else, who succeeded in blocking one state after another from getting membership lists of NAACP state branches, which would certainly have led to the destruction of the branches and of an untold fate for their members.

If Carter was the savior of the NAACP in the southern

states, he was also surely the dominant force in the movement to dismantle de facto segregation in the public schools of the North and West. Again, more than anyone else, Carter and his staff confronted those districts with segregated schools and exposed them to the embarrassing realization that they had much in common with the southern school districts. He was relentless in this crusade and contributed much to the view that the task of eradicating racism was not a sectional one but a truly national one.

Carter's story is the remarkable one of success in the classic sense. Beginning as a shy, diffident youngster, he displayed courage desegregating the swimming pool in the public school he attended that would presage his conduct in later years. As he made his way up the ladder of success to the point that most lawyers regard as the topmost rung, a federal judgeship, he continued to display the equanimity, disarming frankness, courage, and determination that make him the stalwart figure that we all admire.

John Hope Franklin
November 2004

*Chapter 1*

# Early Years

I was born on March 11, 1917, in Careyville, Florida, which is in the Panhandle section of the state, near Pensacola. My mother, Annie Martin Carter, was there awaiting my birth. My father, Robert Lee Carter, had migrated north to take a job in a manufacturing plant in Newark, New Jersey. My mother joined him six weeks after my birth. I was the youngest of nine children, one of whom had died in childbirth, so that we were eight children in the family when we became part of the vanguard of the first great migration of blacks out of the rural South to the industrial North, seeking a better life and freedom from the strictures of southern segregation and discrimination.

Although I left the South when I was only six weeks old, my southern roots are deep. All the people to whom I have known blood ties are from the South, even though they too eventually relocated outside the region. During the years when we lived on Boyden Street in Newark, New Jersey, all the black adults I knew were displaced southerners. Southern black culture was embedded in me. Even now, for example, I find myself, particularly during holiday seasons, craving foods that rural southern blacks regard as appropriate for the occasion: black-eyed peas, rice, chicken, hogshead cheese, and barbecued ribs. Yet, like most of my generation of blacks raised in the North, I am more alienated from whites than are black southerners of my generation.

For the first ten years of my life we lived on Boyden Street, on the second and third floors of a three-story building. The apartment entrance was at the top of a long, narrow stairway that went from street level up the side of the building. There was no central heating or in-door plumbing. There was a public outhouse about a hundred yards from the back of the building. Our only heat was supplied by a coal-burning stove in the kitchen, and during winter much of the time was spent close to it. We bathed about once a week in a tub in the kitchen filled with water heated on the stove.

My father died when I was a year old, and the trauma of his death almost destroyed my mother. My mother had more than a rudimentary education. She could read and write well and was strong and intelligent, but with my father's death and eight children to take care of, she was immobilized. She had no marketable skills and had ex-pected to be a housewife. With this tragic turn of events she simply did not know what to do. After several weeks her sister Lena came from Wilmington, North Carolina. She brought my mother out of her shock and forced her to face reality—that she had to find work to survive and care for her children. At the time the only work available to a black unskilled woman was to become a domestic servant for white people. Being an indifferent cook and not interested in that skill, the only thing for her was to do the laundry and cleaning for one or more white families. This she did for the next twenty-five years.

I was slow to walk and talk, and when I was about four I developed rickets, apparently from spending too much time indoors without proper nutrition. My aunt Lena came again, and took me to live with her in North Carolina for about six months. She lived in a one-family house with an open porch on one side. Every day she would rub my legs with butter and have me lie on the porch in the sun. When we returned to Newark, my legs were strong and straight.

My aunt was annoyed, however, by my unaggressiveness. I would not fight back when set upon by other boys. I did not become physically aggressive until I was in Franklin Elementary School when I was about twelve years old, and a bully—a white boy—gave me no choice. We were in a class in printing. You had to insert a blank page on the pincers and remove your hand as the two pincers came together to print words on the inserted page. I was awkward and slow and always afraid that my hand would be caught and crushed. My terror was evident to everyone in the class. One of the white boys apparently decided that he would show that I was really a sissy, so he opened his pants and rubbed his genitals against my behind. I turned on him in anger and desperation, and beat him up. He was bigger than I and much better developed physically, and he should have given thin-chested, scared me a sound thrashing. I knew nothing of boxing and had not learned how to fight. But this was a kid who wanted to gain points from his buddies at my expense. He was as surprised as I that I did not accept this humiliation; he was a coward, as many bullies seem to be. I was never picked on again, and I cannot recall being in a physical fight since. The experience helped shore up my mental toughness and showed me that I could not let people pick on me or intimidate me. Even though I might suffer a beating, I could not let people walk over me without my making some verbal or physical protest.

Shortly after my return to Newark from Aunt Lena's home, I was severely burned when I tipped over a pot of hot water on the kitchen stove. I was tying my shoes close to the stove, and as I got off my knees my head hit the protruding handle of a pot of boiling water. My sister pulled me back in time so that the water fell only on my legs. I remember being rushed to the hospital in a police van with sirens blasting.

After recovering I enrolled in the Burnett Street School. There were only a few blacks in my classes, and no black boys. The teachers were all white women, but I do not recall experiencing any overt racism at Burnett. I took to school. I liked to read and apparently was a skillful test taker. The teachers encouraged and pushed me, skipping me several grades. This enabled me to graduate from high school at age sixteen.

As a child I discovered the Newark Public Library, which was a short distance from my home, and I began to spend time there reading books for pleasure. This was a totally undisciplined, undirected exercise, but even hap-hazard reading helped expand the mind of a poor, naive, gullible boy with no knowledge of the larger world.

One incident in the school I have never forgotten. It probably shows that even at a young age I was becoming a student of race differentiation and discrimination. Two girls in my sixth-grade class, one white and one black, were good friends. The white girl had long, straight hair that fell over her face and caused her to keep tossing her hair out of her eyes. The black girl mirrored her friend's gesture, although her hair was braided and tightly pinned to the top of her head. (In later years when I became fa-miliar with Mamie and Kenneth Clark's tests with white and black dolls, designed to show that racial discrimina-tion harmed black children at an early age, I was re-minded of these two children.) The two girls later had a falling out, and the white girl complained to the teacher about something the black girl had done. The teacher ex-pressed no sympathy, but told her it served her right be-cause she should stay with her own kind.

During this time my mother was once again racked with grief. My three oldest siblings—Georgia, Arrington, and Beatrice—were all stricken with respiratory infec-tions and died over a span of eighteen months. Georgia was twenty-two, Arrington was twenty, and Beatrice was eighteen. They had been most directly affected by my father's death, especially my oldest brother, Arrington, who had become a street person whom my mother could not control. He had no job and made money gambling. He hung out with a rough group of men. I remember him vaguely as a high-strung guy who would erupt in violence with little warning. My oldest sister, Georgia, was unhappily married, and had two boys, James and Fred. James, the older boy and the apple of her and my mother's eye, died of meningitis shortly before the death of Georgia. Beatrice was the most physically attractive member of our family, outgoing and fun loving, and loved by us all. She was the last of the three to die, and her death broke the family's heart.

I assumed the three had been infected with tuberculosis, and for a long time I felt we were all doomed to die from it.

Newark is now in the throes of massive construction, beautifying the city, but at the time, Boyden Street was becoming one of the worst black slums in the country. In the ten years I lived there it was a poor, racially mixed neighborhood. Italian families still lived there, but they were steadily leaving. From the time I was seven years old, more and more blacks from the rural South began moving in. When the weather was pleasant, large groups of young men would gather on the street near where we lived and try to flirt with the girls and young women as they passed by. With two girls at or nearing puberty, my mother was anxious to move.

This black southern influx after World War I changed the neighborhood. Life pulsed on the street. There was singing, laughter, games, and partying. Saturday night was the men's time to relax by drinking and gambling. Arguments and fights often ensued, a number of which I viewed from our front window. There were no guns then. Knives were the usual weapons. I developed a greater aversion to knives than guns, perhaps because I saw so much blood from knife wounds. One evening I witnessed a man beating another to a bloody pulp with the hard rim of a straw hat.

A fundamentalist religious congregation also came to the neighborhood and opened a storefront church. The church was not associated with any of the major Christian denominations. We called them "foot washers." Their services were held on Saturday. They made beautiful music with tambourines and a choir. I spent so much time at these services that many of my mother's friends thought I was headed for the ministry. But I was there only for the music; as soon as the preaching began, I would leave.

After the death of the three oldest children, our family stabilized. My now-oldest living sister, Mamie, was a skilled seamstress and made clothes. That occupation meant she was at home all the time to keep an eye on the three youngest of us—Alsadene, Alma, and me. John, my older brother, was a young adult and was rarely at home. He may not have finished high school before going to work. He was good-looking, dressed well, and had plenty of girlfriends. He always kept a steady job and eventually settled down with one woman. We were a closely knit family. John was around regularly, watching out for the girls and me, but since he lived outside our home, my closest siblings were my sisters.

The women in my family largely influenced my child-hood development. My mother was a religious woman, and she attended a Baptist church. The preacher gave fiery sermons, and some of the women were moved to shout and swoon. My mother never engaged in that kind of emotional display, but neither was she rigid in her beliefs. Ours was a relaxed, easygoing household. She did believe, however, in a double standard, and I had far fewer social restrictions than my sisters. In extended southern-bred families, any adult could punish a child for mischief the adult witnessed, but my mother did not belong to that school. She made clear that if we got into any mischief, it was to be reported to her and she would determine and administer the penalty, if any.

My mother never remarried. After my father's death, her life was her children. She wanted us to succeed and not be forced, as she was, to make a living doing domestic work for other people. All my friends liked my mother, and I would get annoyed sometimes because they would often spend as much time talking and joking with her as with me. She kept abreast of events in the nation and in the world, read the local newspaper, and had a well-honed sense of humor.

Alsadene, the oldest of the three youngest, was very bright. She should have gone to college, but the only thing available was normal school, which turned out teachers. She did not want to teach, so she made no effort to pass the examination for entry into the school. She finished high school and secured a number of low-grade white-collar jobs. When World War II opened up opportunities for blacks, she got a job in the Social Security Administration and rose to a high civil service position there. After Mamie died in 1946, Alsadene moved first to St. Louis and then to Indianapolis. She married Martin Wade, a railroad porter, and they adopted a girl, Mardean. Alsadene and I were very close. We liked the same things and had similar interests.

Alma, the younger sister, did not have the academic capabilities of Alsadene or myself. She could sew and draw and had a sense of style, but could not make a living with those skills. She studied to become an X-ray technician and joined the staff of a hospital in Philadelphia. She married Paul Lawson, a member of the city council of Philadelphia, and bought a house with a separate apartment on the second floor where my mother lived until her death in 1976.

My oldest surviving sister, Mamie, married, and she lived with us with her husband, John. He owned a bar and grill in a town a few miles from Newark. What she and her husband contributed to the household enabled my mother to satisfy her desperate desire to leave Boyden Street. We moved across town to a house with indoor plumbing and central heating. I was able to run hot water in a bathtub and bathe in the privacy of a bathroom. These were new and welcome amenities, but the downside was that I lost all my friends. But this may well have saved me and my younger sisters from disaster, since a number of our girl pals ended up pregnant and some of the boys spent time in jail. Mamie and her husband stayed with us, which is the reason we were able to have a middle-class family lifestyle from about my twelfth year. She held the family together, at what cost to her marriage I can only guess. Shortly after her death in 1946, the family broke up.

Our family made successive moves, each to more affluent surroundings: from Boyden Street (outhouse), to Highland Avenue (central heating, indoor plumbing, electricity) in Newark, to Ninth Avenue in East Orange (while still a flat in a one-family house, far more spacious). While I was in high school we moved to a one-family house on Eppirt Street in East Orange. The house was set back from the street, was fronted by hedges and a grass lawn, and even had a backyard. We lived on two floors and the owner lived on the top floor, which had a separate entrance. Eppirt Street was my address through my college years. The final move was to a more luxurious three-floor house on Berwyn Street, with wood-burning fireplaces, a family room in the cellar, an enclosed front porch, and a large backyard.

When we moved from Boyden Street to Highland Avenue I had to transfer from Burnett Street School, where I had been skipped to the seventh grade, to Franklin Elementary School. My new teacher said she did not believe in skipping. She made clear at the outset that she would make no allowances for me and that she did not think I could meet her standards without having done the second session of sixth-grade work. She was a formidable woman, and I think there might have been some racial stereotyping in her conviction that I would fail. She was fair, however, and eventually accepted the fact that I could and did meet her standards, and passed me on to the next grade. I had no problem doing the work. The teacher was the missionary type and gave me wholehearted support and encouragement, but in the six-week cycles in which we were graded I never was able to rank first in the class. I was always second. The same girl would always beat me out. I

did not like it, but it was not the last time I would be number two scholastically. Such experiences probably helped
keep my ego under control.

Recorded music was just becoming affordable for those
at our economic level, and we purchased a Victrola. My
mother was very close to a married couple who worked as
butler and maid for a wealthy white family. They gave us a
huge number of operatic recordings—Caruso, Melba,
Lehmann, and Schumann-Heink, among others—that
their employer was discarding. Playing these recordings
was my introduction to opera. Although I cannot sing,
opera and I had an instant love affair, and it has been one of
the pleasures of my life. In music-appreciation class at
school, I showed off my newly acquired knowledge by
bringing a sampling of my records to the class one day.
That was a star turn for me.

My eighth-grade teacher, Miss Vogel, ridiculed my aspirations for a college education in my last semester at the
school. Once, we were assigned to write about a book we
had read and tell why we had chosen that book. I had chosen Virgil's *Aeneid.* I wrote that I liked reading ancient history and mythology and that I had chosen *The Aeneid*
because knowledge from such sources would help me get
to college. But I misspelled *college.* She read my paper to
the class with fulsome sarcasm and disdain, pointing out
the error in spelling, but did not identify me as the writer.
We were all convulsed with laughter, me included. Either
my sense of humor or the appreciation of a good performance (which hers certainly was) insulated me from any
adverse effects of this public put-down.

One day I encountered Miss Vogel in downtown

Newark and greeted her without tipping my hat. I did not
know that courtesy. The following school day she gave
one of her stellar comic performances, about young men
greeting ladies with their hats glued to their heads instead
of tipping them. As was her custom she never identified
the culprit when berating one of us. Thus, as with *The
Aeneid* and the college put-down, I was able to enjoy her
performance as much as my classmates. In this case she
taught me a courtesy that I did not know. The feminist
movement has made this largely obsolete, but it was a
mainstream practice then. It was good for me to be famil-
iar with this custom, since even at age eleven, without
knowing it, the mainstream was where I was headed.

On the last day of school, when I informed Miss Vogel
that I had enrolled in the classical college preparatory
curriculum at Barringer High School—Newark's elite
secondary public school at the time—she expressed anger
and impatience. She said I should go to a vocational
school and learn a trade. This was 1928. Blacks were confined to the upper balcony in the downtown Newark
movie houses. The Civil War had brought slavery to its
end only some sixty years before, and my parents were
part of the first generation of blacks in this country born
free. Miss Vogel could not envision blacks as intellectuals.
She and many whites thought Booker T. Washington, not
W.E.B. DuBois, had it right: that the proper role for
blacks was farming, a trade, or some form of manual
labor. I knew I had no manual dexterity or physical skills
and that my only hope for success was in my intellectual
development. For my first several grade cycles at Bar-

ringer, I would bring my report card to Miss Vogel to show her that I had made all As. I think I was trying to convince her I could do the work that I thought she questioned, but I did not realize then that she was not looking at me as an individual.

I had an excellent academic record at Barringer. Although there were some black students in the school, none were in any of my classes. I was never made to feel by any of the teachers, however, that I did not belong in their class. If the principal or any of his assistants saw me in what they regarded as bad company, it was reported to my mother.

The kind of trouble on Boyden Street that could have aborted my future was not present in the Highland Avenue neighborhood we had moved to. This was a middle-class, racially mixed neighborhood. There were no groups of idle young men hanging out ogling the girls, and no street fights. Night was peaceful and quiet—that was the most striking difference between Boyden Street and Highland Avenue.

There were tennis courts in Branch Brook Park, which bordered our neighborhood. Another boy and I got tennis rackets, taught ourselves to play, and eventually became good enough to keep the ball in play long enough for a good workout. We sold our friends on the game so that spending Saturday afternoon on the tennis courts in the park became a regular occurrence. I thought I was a good tennis player and tried out for a place on the high school team—and was beaten so badly and so swiftly that I was in shock. It is difficult to become good at tennis without taking professional lessons, and there was no money for that luxury. Still, I played tennis well into my seventies.

At the end of my second year at Barringer, we moved to East Orange, New Jersey. East Orange High School, unlike Barringer, was not an elite school. There was only one school for all secondary students. East Orange was rife with racial bias. There were many black students, but we were not welcomed. The policy of the school strongly disfavored any interracial mingling of the students. The black students were not placed in separate classes, but we were seated together.

At the time I attended East Orange High (1932–33), it had one of the best swimming teams in the state and would usually win or place high in all statewide competitions. The swimming pool in the school was available to black students only at the close of school on alternate Fridays, by gender. To protect the white children from contamination the blacks might have left in the pool, it was then drained, cleaned, and refilled for the use of white students the following Monday. White students had to pass a swimming test to secure the requisite credits in physical education required for graduation. This test was not required of black students. We could secure the necessary physical education credits without exhibiting skill in swimming.

The physical education class for boys was held three times a week. Typically, all the boys would gather on the gym floor to be led by the instructor in some form of calisthenics for about a half hour. Then the white boys would go to the swimming pool on the lower level to finish the period learning to swim or to improve their swimming skills; the black boys were left on the upper gym floor to finish the period playing basketball or whatever other physical activity was available.

In May 1933, I read in the local newspaper that the New Jersey Supreme Court in a case from Trenton had held that all public school facilities available to white children had to be available to black children as well. Armed with this knowledge, during the next gym class period I joined the white boys when they retired to the swimming pool. The teacher was, of course, surprised, and at first tried to intimidate me by threatening me with expulsion. When that did not work, he pleaded with me to give in because otherwise he would lose his job. I was unmoved, insisting that the supreme court of New Jersey had said I had a right to use the pool when the white boys used it.

At every physical education class thereafter until graduation I went to the pool when the white boys did. I told the other black students about the decision and tried to get the boys in my gym class to join me, but no one did. It was a difficult, emotional effort for me. I could not swim at the time, but at every gym class, choked up and near tears with emotion and defiance, I would get in the pool at its shallow end and cling to the side until the period ended. None of the white boys used the pool with me in it, so there I was clinging to the side of the pool for dear life until the period ended. Rather than open the pool to all students, the school closed the pool the next school year. White-supremacy culture sometimes exacts a terrible toll on whites.

At both the Newark and East Orange schools the contributions of blacks to the country's development were never mentioned. Nothing was said about blacks in music or literature. I believe at that time jazz was considered trash. Black students were led to feel ashamed and deficient because we were the progeny of slaves. Slavery, when referred to at all, was romanticized. Slaves were on the whole happy, contented, well treated, and fed by kind, caring white masters. If left on their own, the slaves were lazy and shiftless, needing the firm guidance of whites to perform unskilled tasks capably. The Reconstruction era was a disaster—incompetent blacks and unscrupulous whites led the South to ruin. John Brown was a bad man. Yet the fact that my teachers in Newark tried to assess black students on their individual performances, while in East Orange the teachers lumped us all together as undesirables, shows the different faces of white-supremacy culture in the United States. I am sure that Newark teachers were no freer of the conventional wisdom of black inferiority to whites than were the teachers in East Orange, but they stood back and tried to assess us as individuals.

In this racially oppressive climate my academic performance suffered badly. I fell from the ranks of the academically gifted at Barringer High to the brink of academic failure at East Orange High. Instead of As, I was getting mostly Ds. Yet I suppose my experience in East Orange toughened me for later battles with racism.

## Chapter 2

# Becoming a Lawyer

I had done so badly in school in my junior year at East Orange High that I had to attend summer school to make up classes and improve grades in order to move on to my senior year. With graduation a year away I had to find some way to get to college. There was very little, if any, money available for that in my family. Rutgers, a state institution, may have been available at low cost, but no one I knew was aware of that.

This lack of information about available opportunities remains a problem for poor blacks today. I am amazed at how uninformed poor blacks are about the availability of low-cost educational opportunities in mainline educational institutions, despite the fact that much of this information is readily available. That, I suppose, is the critical difference between the uninformed poor and the uninformed middle class. The latter can get the information when needed; the former cannot.

Somehow I made contact with a Dr. Alexander, a graduate of Lincoln University in Pennsylvania who had a medical practice in East Orange. He told me about the school and wrote to the school authorities on my behalf. As a result I was admitted on a work scholarship, but would need to cover tuition myself. Fortunately, an elderly black man who was a friend of our family's had taken an interest in me. He was deeply committed to the uplift of the race, and apparently saw me as a potential leader. He generously provided the required $500 for my tuition, and in September 1933 I was off to college.

Lincoln is one of the oldest institutions in the country offering blacks a college education. At the time of my admission, only men were enrolled. The school was staffed almost totally by white professors who for the most part were either former members of the faculty at Princeton University or among its alumni. The president and the administrative staff at Lincoln were white. There were also several black instructors, most notably William Fontaine, virtually cadaverous in appearance, but vigorous and engaging in his attempt to instill in us his love for the permutations of philosophical thought; John Davis, a brilliant young scholar who had just received his master's degree in political science from Columbia when he joined the faculty in my sophomore year to teach political science; and J. Newton Hill, the only black with professional status, who taught English literature and drama.

Those of us entering Lincoln in 1933 represented a new breed of black men. Slavery had officially and legally ended slightly less than seven decades before. Our parents had been born free, the first generation of free black Americans, and like my parents many had been among that first black wave of migration out of the South during World War I. Although most of my classmates were poor and the first in the family to attend college, some had come from middle-class families of teachers, ministers, and physicians.

Lincoln men had a reputation for boorish, undisciplined public conduct generated by the university's all-male environment. The men would get drunk, become violent, beat up other men, and damage property. Lincoln officials had tended to look the other way, making no effort to curb or punish students. Our class regarded the administration's passive acceptance of such conduct as demeaning and patronizing—seemingly based on a view that blacks were basically savages and that their animalistic conduct had to be tolerated. We felt that black college-educated men had an obligation to engage in socially acceptable conduct in public forums. We were not prudes by any means but believed that as black college men we had an obligation to exercise control over our public conduct.

We also took on matters of more substance and importance: we began agitating for more black faculty, and for student participation in the governance of the institution. Our tangling with the administration on these matters furthered our own development. We had not gone to white institutions, where we would have learned how to compete with white men and not be afraid of doing so. Thus, taking on the white administration undoubtedly helped condition us for competition with white men in various roles later in life.

I entered Lincoln at sixteen, naive and unworldly. While I was developing intellectually, I was also necessarily undergoing social development. Lincoln was an entirely new experience: living in a dormitory among classmates, having a roommate, eating with classmates, and engaging in activities with them outside the classroom. Except for holidays away from the institution, the campus was one's world. At a place as isolated as Lincoln, the bonds that tie you to your classmates are very strong and lasting. In these circumstances close friendships necessarily develop. The friendships I made during my years at Lincoln were stronger than any made during any other period in my life, including the army years. Most of my Lincoln buddies have now predeceased me, but we kept up with one another throughout our lives.

Several years after my graduation, I eagerly went back for a visit. The visit was a huge disappointment—the magic I remembered was not there. I then realized that the sublime contentment and joy I had treasured had not come from the campus or the setting but from my relationships with my friends and our interaction with other students and faculty in the setting the campus provided. I returned to the campus to receive an honorary degree in 1965, but I have never again had the urge to return.

These friendships furthered my social growth. My growth in other areas was largely influenced by Hill, Fontaine, and Davis, the three black faculty members. I was raw, unsophisticated, and not well read, but eager to learn.

In addition to teaching English literature, Professor Hill coached the debating team, and taught drama class and put on plays. I had always been shy, with a soft voice that did not project. I joined the debate team, and we debated a number of the colleges close by, such as Haverford and other small schools. This helped me to overcome my shyness and to use my voice, and I became able to make a formal presentation before a large audience. I was also competing with white contemporaries—another experience that helped me maintain a feeling of ease when in white groups and a lack of fear of competing with white men.

Professor Hill also introduced me to the performing and visual arts. I had learned to enjoy opera singing from the trove of Victrola records I had been given, but I had never seen an opera or attended a recital. He and his wife, Louise, took me to the Metropolitan Opera, the Metropolitan Museum of Art, and the Museum of Modern Art—all firsts for me. They had no children at that time—two daughters were born after my time with them. I suppose they were doing for me what they later did for their children. I was a surrogate son of sorts. With the guidance and exposure they provided, the theater, opera, ballet, recitals, and art shows became a part of my life.

Bill Fontaine was a scholar, engrossed in plowing the life of the mind. He thought I had the potential to follow in his footsteps, although I doubt that I possessed the qualities needed to devote oneself to pure scholarship. I am too pragmatic to desert the world for too long. From him, however, I did learn to engross myself in studying various treatises in philosophy and psychology, analyzing their content and cogently articulating what I believed to be their message. He spent most of his time reading, studying, and writing, and tried to impart his love for developing one's mind to his students, especially those he considered promising. He followed my career with the NAACP and approved of the path I had chosen. His approval meant a great deal—more than that of the other two, perhaps because their influence was so evident in my life—because even though I had not devoted myself to scholarship as Fontaine had hoped I would, he still embraced me.

John Davis was both a scholar and a pragmatist. He used his intellect to help devise strategies and activities to fight racial discrimination. He was a native of Washington, D.C., and had authored the plan to boycott the People's Drug Store chain there in the 1930s in a successful effort to force the hiring of black employees. The concerted refusal of blacks to patronize People's Drug Store was the first such action of its kind in the nation and led to a Supreme Court ruling that the Norris–La Guardia Act could not be used to bar peaceful picketing to secure economic or racial gains. John also felt I had the potential for serious intellectual development, and both he and Bill Fontaine encouraged me to go on from Lincoln to graduate or professional school. In my senior year in law school I was awarded a Rosenwald Fellowship, on John's recommendation, I believe. He never acknowledged responsibility, but he was the only possible source.

These three men in a real sense took me in hand and molded me. I was singled out for treatment accorded to no other member of my class. Bill had respiratory problems and died at a relatively young age. Professor Hill lived into his seventies. John died in December 2002 at ninety-one. Of the three men, John—the pragmatist— was to become my role model.

Another influence should be mentioned. In my junior year at Lincoln, William Hastie, who was later to become assistant secretary of the army and the first black to leave such a high position to protest the army's refusal to end segregation, was a guest speaker at the university. He was subsequently the first black governor of the Virgin Islands and the first black appointed to the federal court of appeals, and later became the first chief judge. Hastie was a very distinguished and urbane presence. He was not a spellbinding speaker, which in view of my own limitations in that regard made him a very attractive role model. He made a great impression on me.

I had a good academic record at Lincoln, graduating magna cum laude, second in academic standing in the class. I gave the salutatory commencement address. I had not decided on the future, but I did want to continue my academic studies. In fact, I knew I had to do so, since I lacked physical dexterity, skills, or the desire to teach in the public schools. My tentative career choice was to join the faculty of a college or university. Although I dreamed of developing the elegance seen in Hastie, law did not strike me as a viable option, particularly because I then thought lawyering required spellbinding oratory.

As graduation from Lincoln grew closer, it was clear that there was no money for Harvard or any other main-line academic institution. Fortuitously, the then-current dean of Howard University Law School came to Lincoln recruiting and offered me a scholarship, which, augmented by funds from part-time employment to help take care of room and board, enabled me to attend law school. Thus, my decision to study law was opportunistic. If funds had been available to finance graduate study in political science, history, or even philosophy at Harvard, Columbia, or some such institution, I would certainly have chosen that path.

What made Howard especially intellectually stimulating was that the school was on a special mission.

Charles Houston was a Harvard Law graduate. He believed that equal citizenship rights for blacks was required and guaranteed by the federal Constitution, and he took over the deanship of Howard Law School with the goal of turning out a cadre of black lawyers who would return to their communities and institute test cases challenging on constitutional grounds various forms of discrimination to which blacks were subjected. Until he took over leadership of the school, Howard was unaccredited, with loose academic standards, and operated a night school enabling men and women who held full-time jobs to secure a law degree. A number of these people passed the D.C. bar, and some eventually managed to build a full-time legal practice. Most, however, were never able to do that and had to continue being waiters, postal workers, and porters as full-time occupations.

Houston set out to change all this. He abolished the night school, modeled the curriculum on Harvard's, hired some rigorously trained teachers, mostly black, and within a few years secured accreditation for the school. In every course the legal fundamentals of the subject were taught and mastered, and if an area of discrimination against blacks existed, class discussion centered on possible avenues that might lend themselves to litigation to strike down the barrier. Until this course of study was instituted at Howard, civil rights were not part of the law school curriculum in any law school. It has now become a subject taught in every major law school in the country. Houston trained a generation of civil rights lawyers, the most notable being Thurgood Marshall, who graduated from Howard in 1933. In 1934, Houston became the chief legal counsel for the NAACP, and he soon hired Marshall as his assistant in orchestrating a sustained legal challenge to the segregation system.

In the spring of 1938, during the second semester of my first year, I witnessed Houston's approach firsthand when he prepared and argued the first major school case to reach the Supreme Court, *Missouri ex rel. Gaines v. Canada*. Lloyd Gaines, a black resident of St. Louis, Missouri, had the requisite qualifications and had applied for admission to the University of Missouri Law School. Although the state had no law school for blacks, he was turned down because the school did not admit African Americans. Houston had a dry run of his Supreme Court argument in the law school the day before his scheduled court appearance. The significance of the dry run was that one of the students asked Houston the same question one of the justices put to him the next day. That created an NAACP tradition of its lawyers thereafter making each of their scheduled Supreme Court arguments before the Howard Law School students in advance of the Supreme Court presentation.

I went to the Court, my first time in the Supreme Court, to hear the argument. The building epitomizes the majesty of the law. When the justices took their places on the bench, led by Chief Justice Charles Hughes, an imposing figure, I was very impressed and moved. *Gaines* was the second case to be heard that day. When the case was called and Houston rose to commence his argument, Justice James McReynolds swiveled his chair so that his back was to Houston until he completed his presentation. What strikes me now is that I thought there was nothing unusual about McReynolds's petty and mean discourtesy, and there was no reaction from those in attendance in the Court. I am filled with anger when I now revisit the incident. McReynolds was supposed to represent us all, but at the time blacks were not regarded as being worth consideration.

There is a story about McReynolds in the black community. After the Court ended its session for the day, McReynolds went for a haircut and told his barber, who was black, that he had just heard "that nigger Houston." His barber stopped cutting McReynolds's hair, came around to face him, and said, "Houston has done a great deal of good for Negroes and we think he is a great man, capable of sitting on the Supreme Court, and if he got such appointment he would represent all the people, both whites and Negroes." While the barber spoke, McReynolds sank lower and lower in the chair. When he finished his speech, the barber resumed cutting McReynolds's hair. The story may be apocryphal, but I like to believe it happened.

When I entered Howard, I was strapped financially. I

had to eat breakfast at a Father Devine's soup kitchen, where for 10¢ you were served a hearty breakfast of southern cooking—hominy grits, biscuits, and bacon, ham, or sausage. Before being served you had to swear to the server that you could not afford to eat in a regular restaurant. The question was put with some vigor, but your word was accepted. I needed more income but had no marketable skills. One of the former graduates of the school was asked to help me. He was a waiter in one of the big hotels in D.C. He took me on as a busboy and showed me how to carry food on a tray, and after I was able to manage that, he secured a job for me at one of the hotels to serve dinner. The job was relatively easy and kept me in spending money as well as sufficient funds for other necessary expenses.

I was on the job for a few months in the spring of my second year in law school. That spring Marian Anderson, the noted black mezzo-soprano, was barred from giving a recital at Constitution Hall by the Daughters of the American Revolution. This caused the resignation of a number of women in the organization, the most famous being Mrs. Eleanor Roosevelt. The first lady then arranged for Ms. Anderson to give her recital at the Lincoln Memorial on Easter Sunday.

This was a historic event for the nation and particularly for blacks. I wanted to hear the concert and asked to have the day off. My boss refused. I decided I was not missing the event and joined the thousands of people of both races at the Mall to hear Ms. Anderson sing. It was a beautiful spring day. The atmosphere was charged with excitement. The dominant emotion was reverence and joy, for you knew that you were witnessing a historic event that signaled a new era in race relations. Many of us shed tears; she was a regal presence and in glorious voice.

I went to the restaurant after the concert. The place was in chaos. After the meal was served I was fired, which I had more or less expected. This was the first time I left a job on principle without knowing what I would do next. By that time it was evident that I would be a success academically. I was given a full scholarship, which covered all my expenses, and was paid generously for a few hours' work in the library. My duties were so minimal that for the most part time in the library was used for study.

I graduated from Howard in the spring of 1940. That summer I took a bus trip south. Except for my visit with my aunt in Wilmington, I had not been south, and I wanted to see what it was like. I remember very little about that trip, except an incident that occurred as I headed back north. I was traveling by bus from Tallahassee, Florida, and had an altercation with the police in Waycross, Georgia, for refusing to give up my seat to a white passenger. I was dragged off the bus, called "one of those smart niggers from New York," and threatened. I disclaimed any connection with New York, saying I was from Washington and had just finished law school and was just making a trip south. Perhaps the law school part gave them pause; they let me get back on the bus and, surprisingly, I was not beaten up, which was the usual result of these encounters. Interestingly, all the other passengers had been put on another bus, and I was the only passenger on the bus to its final destination in Newark, New Jersey. I had been very calm and composed in the confrontation with the police, but when the bus began rolling I collapsed, and the driver had to stop to allow me to relieve myself. I knew I was extremely lucky to be in one piece. Segregation was not new to me. I had attended school in Washington for three years, but during this trip to the Deep South I was exposed to the arbitrary nature of white enforcement of black subservience. I do not believe I told my family about my scary adventure until enough time had elapsed for me to make a good story out of it and make it seem less terrifying to them than it had actually been for me.

During my last year at Howard, I was awarded a Rosenwald Fellowship, which I used to pursue additional work at Columbia University. At the time, in my judgment, the essential preservative of the democratic ingredients of our society was the First Amendment—freedom to speak, to write, and to join forces with others to advance programs and policies without regard to government approbation or disapproval. I applied for admission to Columbia's law graduate school and requested that Professor Noel Dowling, then a national authority on constitutional law, be my faculty adviser. I had graduated from Howard magna cum laude and my three-year academic record consisted mostly of As with an occasional B. It never occurred to me that I would not be accepted. Weeks went by, however, without any reply. Finally, losing patience, I wrote another letter demanding an answer, acceptance or rejection. That brought a response accepting my application for admission.

Some weeks later I went to the school to meet the dean of the graduate school. The interview was infuriating.

The dean made clear that he doubted I could meet the school's academic standards. He recognized that I had done well at Howard but dismissed that, since he did not place Howard on Columbia's lofty academic perch. He advised me that I had two choices. I could enroll in the program for a doctorate in juridical science, which would require a one-year residence at the school. Few courses would be required. Most of my time would be devoted to doing research and writing my thesis. At the end of the year's residence I could submit my partially completed thesis, and if it was of high quality I would be awarded a master's degree. If I wished to pursue a doctorate at that point, I would then be given five additional years to complete the thesis, and be awarded the doctorate if the thesis was found to be acceptable. Patronizingly, he advised me against taking that route. I did not give the matter a moment's thought. I told him I would pursue the doctorate program.

I enrolled in Columbia in the fall of 1940. My residency began with a distasteful and disrespectful incident. All students in the graduate program were assigned cubicles in the library. Instead of being given a cubicle on the mezzanine, I was assigned a table in the basement, alone amid stacks of books. For a few days it did not dawn on me what was happening, but when I realized, I protested. I was then assigned a desk in one of the cubicles, to be shared with two other graduate students, a man who was rarely in evidence and a woman from Oregon. When I saw the setup, I understood my previous Siberian assignment—which undoubtedly stemmed from concern that I would be alone in the isolated area and might make unwanted advances on the woman. Obviously, none who initially approved the basement assignment told me this, but the law faculty at the time had a decidedly southern accent.

Interestingly, the woman was a very nice person. She did not seem to feel threatened by being alone in my company so much of the time. In fact, she appeared to welcome the opportunity to air some of her most personal problems. I am sure she did this with confidence that she could make these revelations with impunity, since I had no access to her circle, where disclosure of some of these intimate tidbits would cause her embarrassment.

My faculty adviser, Professor Dowling, was an Alabaman. I knew nothing of this or his social views. My information was that he was an authority on constitutional law; I should have found out more about him before selecting him as my faculty adviser. It was obvious from our initial interview that he was uncomfortable. Columbia had very few black law students, and I am reasonably certain that I was the first black enrolled in the graduate department, and that Dowling had never before dealt with a black scholar on a one-to-one basis. His basic conviction was that I was not up to the task.

I wrote my thesis on the essentiality of the First Amendment for the preservation of a democratic society. When I presented him with parts of my thesis, his comments were always negative: my writing was deficient; the idea development was not clear. Each of his criticisms I would challenge, and he would back down. This went on for the entire year. Finally, a week before the school term was to end, at what was to be our last encounter, he approved my thesis. In parting, he said that he had to admire my persistence; that despite his litany of criticisms, I had refused to be discouraged. Then he said, revealingly, that he hoped I did not think that because he was from Alabama, his criticisms or negative reactions were the result of racial prejudice. I assured him that I had no such feeling.

Despite Dowling, I was confident that my product was up to standard. His approval, however, gave me no joy. I filed the thesis away and didn't look at it again for some sixteen years. In 1957, while seeking to resist the effort of the state of Alabama to secure the names and addresses of NAACP members, I reviewed the document and the research done in connection with it. On the basis of my thesis work, I developed the argument that the First Amendment's right to freedom of assembly protected the identities of the rank-and-file members of the NAACP from being disclosed to the state, since such disclosure would interfere with their right to join with others to engage peacefully in activities that the state sought to outlaw.

Aside from the racial issue, Dowling and I were at odds over how we viewed the law. He thought the about-face of the United States Supreme Court in reference to Roosevelt's New Deal policies was based solely on technical differences between the proposals that had been disapproved and those now found to be acceptable. I believed the Court's about-face was caused by political considerations. Around this time President Roosevelt's attempt to enact his New Deal legislation had met with fierce resistance on the Court. His threat to pack the Court in 1937, more than anything else, caused the Court to soften its stance and to approve his legislation. I took Dowling's constitutional law course, and we engaged in a running argument about this.

Fortunately, I retained enough knowledge of Dowling's technical approach to use it in urging the Court in *Brown v. Board of Education* that precedent was not an impediment to their finding that *Plessy v. Ferguson*'s separate but equal doctrine had no application to education, since it had initially been applied in a railroad case. Although the doctrine's applicability to education had been assumed, I argued, it had never been considered in that context by the Court. That opportunity was being presented for the first time in *Brown*, where we argued that the Court should hold that the doctrine had no application to education and should be overruled. Chief Justice Earl Warren bought the argument and articulated it in his opinion for the Court.

My confidence in my thesis was vindicated. Several years later, after the end of World War II, I was urged by Columbia faculty to complete my thesis, and my time to do so was extended five years. But it was too late. I had been seared into zealotry by the humiliations suffered in the armed services and had pledged all my time and energy to the fight against racial discrimination.

I made a number of friends who were second- and third-year law students. There was tension between liberals and leftists. Socialism and Communism were very attractive concepts for a poor black intent on securing the benefits available to similarly situated white men. Communism professed dedication to equal rights and benefits for all without racial barriers. Two factors probably kept me from joining the Communist Party. First, I resist signing up to join anything—but that could have been overcome. More important, my basic problem with the American Communist Party or the members I encountered was that their views were governed and controlled by the Soviet Union. I regarded myself as a loyal American, and I did not believe my social and political views should be based on those of a foreign power, particularly if those views were at odds with American interests. The explanation that it was essential to the cause that the Soviet Union be preserved satisfied me not at all. I am certain that the Left's alliance with Soviet policy undermined the liberal movement in this country, allowing conservatives to lump all liberal thinkers with Communists and tarnish all with the label of a lack of patriotism at best and usually with treason.

I had a very good time at Columbia. I don't think there were any black students in the law school at that time. My friends were white law students and I maintained lifelong friendships with several of these men, including Alan Brodsky, Bob Konove, Justin Feldman, and Herb Prashker. I didn't know very much about Harlem; I was a country bumpkin from East Orange. Every two weeks or so, I'd have to go back home to be with black folks, and get some collard greens and southern food. My social relationships with my friends at Columbia, though, were so warm and free of racial inhibition that I had really begun to believe that race discrimination was not a factor to be given serious consideration. My classes were fascinating. While I openly disagreed with Dowling's views, I enjoyed his class, and the grades given were fair. And the Dowling negativism was negated when the faculty urged me to finish the dissertation so that I could receive the doctorate. I have often wondered whether my life would have taken a different path had I had a different adviser. I might have pursued a career in academia instead of civil rights.

What is interesting is that while I felt the school's treatment of me was racially motivated, it took years for me to become angry about the way I was dealt with at the time. For a time after becoming a judge, I was on various committees for the Columbia University Law School to provide diversity. Then I began to decline because there were other black alumni the school could turn to. For the past ten years, however, my memories have turned to anger and resentment. The long delay in responding to my application, the arrogance and patronizing treatment in the initial interview, the relegation to the basement— all were part of the pattern of race in America that blacks had to tolerate. Now, of course, similar treatment is unacceptable.

I was awarded my master of laws degree in the spring of 1941. That summer I was at loose ends. The year at Columbia had not been as satisfactory as I had hoped. I had my degree, but the good feeling I had expected had eluded me. While certain that Dowling had not judged me fairly, there was some nagging, underlying uncertainty.

I had been protected by my family from some social experiences that most black males of twenty-four had undergone. While not a virgin and not totally lacking in some skill in dealing with women, my experience was

quite limited. Yet two girls I liked being with began pressing for a permanent commitment that I was not ready to
give. I had been in school of some kind since I was six
years old and I wanted a respite from academia. I was dis-
satisfied but had no clear idea of what to do about it. I did
not want to get married; I knew I was not ready to take
that step.

I made no effort to resist the draft. Indeed, I welcomed
it. Temporarily, it enabled me to evade my problems, particularly the pressure for marriage. I thought army service
would make me physically stronger and healthier, provide
new and different experiences, and help me focus more
clearly on what I should do with my life. It did so, but in a
manner I could not have foreseen. In August 1941, I was
inducted into the armed services and had my first confrontation with raw, crude racism. It was the army experience that made a militant of me. It instilled in me a fierce
determination—a zealousness—to fight racism with all
my intellectual and physical strength.

## Chapter 3

# Jim Crow Army

I was inducted into the armed forces in August 1941. We were not officially in the war, although we were supplying Britain with necessary goods and services to enable it to survive. While I did not enter the services with any great patriotic fervor—the army was segregated and I wondered whether as a black my intelligence would be put to any good use—I really wanted to become an effective and capable cog in the military effort.

On induction our initial assignment was roughly six weeks' orientation and training at Fort Dix, New Jersey. Fort Dix was not much of a shock. Being crowded in one room with so many men was new, but in my first year in college I had shared a toilet and shower with all the men on my floor in the dormitory, so the common latrine was not for me the shock it was for many recruits. We drilled and performed various calisthenics, and were taught to stand tall, salute, and make our beds in the army style. One of the recruits in my group was a childhood acquaintance from Boyden Street. Joshua Coston had had some minor encounters with law enforcement, but nothing major. He was very pleasant and outgoing, and we enjoyed reminiscing about our childhood escapades. But although we were in the same unit for about six months, our paths since childhood had been so diverse that we had to look to others for an ongoing relationship.

At the end of our six-week Fort Dix orientation, we were sent to an air base in Augusta, Georgia, as members of the Army Air Corps. The group consisted of men from New Jersey, New York, Pennsylvania, and Kentucky—all of us black. We were a reasonably well educated group of black men for that time. Most of the men were high school graduates, some had college degrees, and one or two had graduate degrees. With a graduate law degree, I had the highest academic credentials of the group.

We were introduced to the armed services' racist culture immediately on arrival. Before we were allowed to shed our duffel bags and be assigned sleeping quarters, we were lined up to receive our commander's welcoming remarks. And quite a welcome it was. He was a middle-aged white captain and was accompanied by a grisly black man with a lot of stripes on his sleeve that I later learned were those of a master sergeant—the highest rank for an enlisted man.

The captain introduced himself. I do not remember his name, and I think I never absorbed it, since what he said was so chilling and he was rarely around. He greeted us by saying that he had studied our personnel files and wanted to inform us right away that he did not believe in educating niggers. He was not going to tolerate our putting on airs or acting uppity. To him we were just niggers and as long as we understood that we would get along fine. With that he turned us over to the sergeant. Evidencing black resilience, or indeed that of any oppressed people, there was no moaning or groaning or any discussion among us about his remarks after we were dismissed. Most of us were thinking that we had to find the way to survive. I do not remember ever speaking to the captain during my time in Augusta. I can see the sergeant now in my mind's eye, but the captain draws a blank.

We received precious little military training. We were given a few lessons in how to load and dismantle a rifle, but the lessons were so rudimentary that I was never able to dismantle a rifle and put it back together until I went to officer candidate school about six months later. We were not marched or drilled regularly. We were not required to perform group calisthenics regularly, nor were our bunks subjected to daily inspection like at Fort Dix. We were awakened at six in the morning by a bugle call, lined up to answer roll call, dismissed to have breakfast, and lined up again after breakfast for work details, which consisted mostly of clearing brush on the base. This was hard manual labor, and I was determined that I was not going to spend my time doing that, having spent some twenty years in school to avoid having to perform that kind of chore.

The sergeant was a nearly illiterate career soldier. He was among that group of poor blacks who had joined the armed services in their teens and served the role the racist military viewed as appropriate for blacks, servants to white officers when not enrolled in the few all-black units in existence when the country was not on a war footing. In 1941, with a large number of civilian blacks being drafted, these black career military men who had served chiefly as household servants of white officers were now assigned as ranking enlisted men to oversee the training of the black civilian recruits under the ultimate supervision of the white officers in charge. Our captain must have been a military dud, which was the reason he was assigned to us.

The military in 1941 did not see blacks as capable fighting men. The memory of the military was highly selective on that issue. It did not remember that 180,000 free blacks and runaway slaves had fought with valor in the Union army during the Civil War to secure their freedom from slavery. It did not remember that blacks had fought with distinction in the Spanish-American War and in World War I, albeit in segregated units. My unit was formed at the outset of the war effort and operated with the southern-oriented mind-set that then dominated the thinking of the military brass, which had no idea what to do with all these black draftees.

The sergeant learned that I was a lawyer, or at least to him I was. I had not taken the New York bar exam and was not admitted to practice in any state. I had, of course, a surplus of legal training, sufficient to be of service to the sergeant and for me to avoid the backbreaking chore of clearing brush. The sergeant had some messy personal problems. He had several girlfriends and was married to a number of women at the same time. Being the sergeant's lawyer, I was assigned a desk in the clerk's office, and my duty was to read and respond to the sergeant's personal mail and to give him legal advice on the handling of his affairs with his various women. That was my mission until December 1941, shortly after Pearl Harbor, when our unit was sent to the Port of New York for shipment overseas.

When we arrived in New York, it was discovered that we had no real military training. The black community was becoming increasingly outspoken about discrimination. The military was on the hot seat about the use of black troops and the lack of black officers, and for having no plan to provide blacks with any opportunity to become officers or receive elite military training, all of which must have made the military brass have second thoughts about sending us overseas.

Whatever the reason, the order to embark for an overseas destination was canceled, and we were sent back to Augusta. Civilian agitation had in the interim borne fruit, and officer candidate schools were now open to blacks. On my return to Augusta I applied for such an assignment, and in January 1942 I was assigned to quartermaster corps officer candidate school in Virginia. I left Augusta to enter another phase of my armed services career.

The assignment involved six weeks of classes, mostly academic courses. The school was integrated—the instructors were all white officers, but the students were black and white. I believe there were about ten black men in a group of about sixty men. We were housed in tents, and my memory is that all ten black recruits were housed together in one of the tents. We were taught how to fire and dismantle a rifle, marched in formation daily, and given stretching and strength-building calisthenics to perform daily too. We also had to go on a long march designed for endurance. Some of the exercises pushed me to the limits of my strength, but each time I thought I would have to cry uncle and drop out, a halt was called. We learned that the mission of the quartermaster corps was to funnel provisions and supplies, but I do not remember any concentration on the specifics of our function as officers. It was a very pleasant interlude, and my health improved immeasurably. I had been thin-chested and subject to constant respiratory ailments, but in that environment I gained weight and some chest depth and had fewer colds and sniffles. Although blacks were housed separately, we did mingle with whites in the classrooms and at meals, so some pleasant superficial relationships did develop among the men in the two groups.

At the end of the six-week tour, we received our second lieutenant bars and our initial duty assignment in our new role. I was assigned to Harding Field in Baton Rouge, Louisiana. I was the only black officer on the base. I was assigned to a company of black men that was among a group of companies keeping supplies moving to frontline fighter pilot squadrons. The commanding officer was white and pleasant enough, but our relationship was minimal. He had a fancy car and spent most of his time off the base enjoying the delights of the town.

I learned there was an officers' club on the base and decided to use it. The club was located in a fair-sized room with a bar across the back end. I had to traverse the length of the room to get to the bar. The room had a good number of white men present—officers, I assumed—and my entry was greeted with complete silence. Walking to the bar amid that silence was for me akin to walking a gauntlet. The bartender was a black man who on seeing me looked as frightened as I felt. I ordered a scotch and soda. He said he did not believe he could serve me. I asked if this was an officers' club, and, pointing to my second lieutenant bars, I told him he could see I was an officer, could he not, and to please let me have the drink. He fixed the drink. When I attempted to pay cash, my performance was ruined. He could not accept cash, only chips. When I was about to wilt, one of the men at the bar told him to put it on his bill. I thanked the officer, and managed to get the glass to my mouth without my hand shaking. I took what I considered a reasonable time to finish the drink and then left, trying to exhibit a calm and dignity I did not feel. I remained on the base about a week after that incident, but I could not muster the resolve to try again.

Being single, I was assigned to a dormitory for visiting officers on the base; being the only black officer, I was housed in the dormitory with other officers. A few nights after the bar episode, having completed my nightly ablutions, I headed for bed. The corridor was dimly lit. I was in my pajamas, and a white man, evidently a newly arrived officer, asked me about hangers. I suppressed an initial impulse to offer a few of mine and instead responded in the negative. He became agitated and said this was one hell of a place. I laughed and told him I could not agree more. He then yelled, "Don't get uppity with me, nigger!" I responded, "Get out of my face with that nonsense," and continued on to my room. He then yelled,

"Who is this nigger?" Someone must have told him I was a second lieutenant, because shortly after his outburst, he came to my room. As he closed in on me, I saw he wore the bars of a lieutenant colonel. He said to me, "I am your senior officer by many grades, and when you speak to me you say sir." I said, "I will say sir to you when you learn some manners. Now get the hell out of my room." He left. The next morning when I went to the latrine to wash up, he was there shaving with only his shorts on. Seeing me, all the visible parts of his body turned a deep red, and he hurriedly left.

Later that day I was summoned to the office of the base commander, a brigadier general. He told me I was about to start a riot. In a separate incident, I had had court-martial charges drawn up against two white enlisted men who had been disrespectful to me. As a second lieutenant, certain protocols were required, which they had ignored. They would not salute me, and would laugh when I threatened to press charges. They were showing plainly that because I was black, my rank did not mean a thing to them. So the base commander had three incidents in mind when he spoke of rioting. I demurred. I told him that I insisted on my officer status being respected. He spoke about how he sympathized because he was from Vermont, but he wanted me to move off the base. I would receive an extra allowance for that, a stipend available only to married officers. I refused. I told him I was not en-titled to live off base as a single officer and I was not going to do so voluntarily. I told him he could order me off the base, but the uniform I wore was going to be respected even if I had to appeal to Washington. All this seems very resolute, but it was far from that in the doing. In these situations, my eyes fill with tears; my voice breaks; and instead of showing the strength and courage I would like, I come across as on the verge of collapse. What I make myself do, with the tears about to fall, voice quavering, is keep my eyes level with whomever I must until the episode is mercifully over.

A few days later I had orders transferring me to Lockridge Air Base in Columbus, Ohio. There was another black officer there and we were housed together. That was a pleasant interlude. There was a sizable middle-class black community in Columbus, so there was good social life with women and men who were attending or were graduates from Ohio State.

Yet even there race had its day. I became a member of the base judge advocate's staff and was assigned to defend a black soldier under court-martial charges for raping a white woman. A black American man has been conditioned to view such claims with deep skepticism. I felt the soldier was probably not guilty. His story was that they had been having sex regularly, but they had a fight over her fee, and she claimed she had been raped. Another soldier said he had had sex with the woman for a fee as well. At the hearing I was able to shake her up so that she did not come across as a credible witness. The testimony of the defendant and his friend that she was in fact a prostitute apparently convinced the panel, and the charges were dismissed.

Instead of being congratulated for vindicating an innocent man, the local judge advocate was furious, apparently preferring to believe that no white woman would have sex with a black man except under coercion. I was summarily removed from the judge advocate's staff. I became something of a hero to the black enlisted men on the base and would have had a sizable defense practice had I stayed on the base.

After a few months in Columbus, however, we were ordered to New York for shipment overseas. Then the supply or quartermaster officers for the various units involved were sent to Norfolk, Virginia, to secure the required supplies for each of their units. The group consisted of about six men. I was the lone black. We were not housed in a military installation, but had to eat and find housing in the town. This meant that while we worked together during the day, I had to find food and shelter apart from the others because of segregation. Nonetheless, we seemed to have become a closely knit group by the time our mission was accomplished, and we headed back to our units. On the trip out of Norfolk, I was offered some evidence of the fact that my racial and color difference had been only temporarily forgotten. One of the men whom I found the most engaging of the lot had tied his sweater on the outside of his duffel bag, and it was gone when he retrieved the bag to disembark from the ferry. He said, "Some stupid, thieving nigger probably stole it." As soon as he said it, he and the rest remembered that I was not white. The silence was deadening. I felt humiliated and was unable to comment. Shortly thereafter we ended the trip, and I never saw these men again. I was more embarrassed by my defeatist reaction than by the racist remarks. I had certainly heard such remarks many times before, but it took several more such experiences before I was able to respond in an appropriately cold or cutting way.

When I returned to my unit, instead of continuing on with it, I was ordered to report to the adjutant general's school in Maryland for another six weeks' training. On completion of that assignment I was sent to Tuskegee, Alabama, to join a supply group training to provide supplies for the 332nd Fighter Squadron—the black pilot group over which Colonel (later General) Benjamin Davis Jr. was put in command. One of the pilots, Creston Gleed, had been a fellow student in my first year in law school. We had become good friends, but Gleed had not been ready for law school study. He wanted adventure. He decided to sign on as a sailor on a merchant ship and almost persuaded me to go with him, but I was not ready for that kind of exotic adventure. He became a very good pilot, survived the war, settled in California, and eventually finished law school and practiced law. He was at Tuskegee along with several other college acquaintances.

From Tuskegee we moved to Seldfridge Field just outside Detroit and then to Alpena, Michigan, for final training before shipping out to Europe. I had a very active social life both on and off the field. You bond very closely with the men in your unit because you are scheduled to face danger and possible death together soon. I was seen by my buddies as totally naive, and they deemed themselves with their more extensive experience as my protectors against unworthy females. I had enough sense of self-preservation to protect myself if needed, but they did not think so. They were always trying to make sure that I enjoyed the company of the various women I dated but that there be no permanent commitment. I had some very pleasant relationships with several women, and my bond with a woman from Texas was very strong, but commitment was avoided. I liked her very much, but she came into my parlor a number of years before I was ready to take on the responsibility of family.

In early 1944, my oldest surviving brother, John, whom we called Dearie, died, and I was granted a furlough to go home to attend the funeral. This was the first death in the family since my childhood when my three oldest siblings had sickened and died in an eighteen-month span, and it seemed that all of us were destined to die young of tuberculosis. The family's health had stabilized for the next twenty years. Dearie was about fifteen years older than I and began living apart from the rest of the family when I was ten or eleven years old. He was a gentle, good-hearted man and would try intermittently to guide me to maturity, but he was not around often enough to be of much help. We were certainly fond of each other but not sufficiently bonded to make his passing the wrenching emotional experience it might have been.

I do not really know how or why during the assignment in Michigan I got off on the wrong foot with my superior officers, all of whom were white, except for one major who could and did pass for white at times off base. The senior officers in charge felt the need to get through the racial curtain. Still, they were less concerned with parting the curtain on their own than with recruiting men to put the finger on malcontents—those complaining about discrimination. When I was interviewed, the message I heard was that they wanted me to report to the commander all would-be troublemakers and activities that could cause problems—in other words, to be their snitch. Not only wasn't I prepared to take on that assignment, but I would probably be among those most likely to complain about orders we considered unfair.

When it was found that I would not be coming to them with tales about my colleagues, I became suspect. There might have been several other reasons for this. *PM*, a liberal New York newspaper, was being sent to me through the mail, which in the eyes of some military personnel made me a dangerous leftist. I was the most educated man in the group and black, had a history of confrontation in Louisiana, and had secured the dismissal of charges against a black man for raping a white woman, all of which may have made me appear dangerous and unreliable. This is all speculation. I do not know the cause, but when my unit left Michigan for its overseas assignment as the 332nd supply group, I was left behind with five other officers under a Major Hayes's command.

We remained in Alpena through April 1944 and did nothing constructive. Hayes had us out marching every day and issued stupid orders that he probably expected us to disobey. Our disobedience resulted in demerits. Indeed, the whole purpose of the exercise was apparently for him to compile on each of us a profile evidencing malingering and refusal to obey superiors, and to find that in attitude, temperament, and personality we were not officer material.

In or about April 1944, we were ordered to report to Fairfield Air Base in Dayton, Ohio, for an administrative hearing. The result was a foregone conclusion. The purpose of the hearing was to demote us as officers and make us available to our respective draft boards for induction into the armed services as enlisted men. This would be accomplished by our being discharged from service with neither an honorable nor a dishonorable discharge, either category making us not subject to the draft. By this exercise, we were being demoted from officer status to enlisted men.

I came home in May 1944, not knowing what to do or where to turn. I was very depressed and discouraged. For a time I was completely indolent and did nothing constructive. I would hang around the house in East Orange all day and spend the nights at parties in Newark or New York, having intimacies with as many women as I could. I did stir myself to get a job as a clerk in some manufacturing company in Newark to finance my nights on the town. Finally, I decided I could not just go to pieces. I had to make some attempt to fight. I called Bill Hastie, then dean of Howard Law School. He agreed to see me. I went to Washington with considerable trepidation because I had not jumped to obey every ridiculous order Hayes had issued and I worried that Hastie might find me at fault. Fortunately for me, Hastie became angry when he read the record on which the administrative discharge was based. He thought I had been treated badly and unfairly and agreed to represent me before the Army Discharge Review Board to get my discharge changed to honorable. That lifted a heavy load off my mind. I returned home with energy and purpose. I decided to study for the October 1944 New York bar examination. I sold my car, quit my job, and spent the next few months immersed in reviewing New York law. I had a room in a friend's apartment in Harlem, but decided that my room at my mother's house in East Orange would prove less distracting.

I took the bar examination on October 25 and 26, 1944. On October 28, 1944, upon Bill Hastie's suggestion, I wrote to Walter White applying for appointment to the NAACP legal staff. In the letter I set forth my credentials. On November 13, 1944, I received a response from Thurgood Marshall saying my letter had been referred to him and that I should come to the office at 11:30 Friday morning, November 17, for a conference with Mr. White and him. Mr. White did not make the conference. Thurgood told me to call Walter and try to see him before he left for a two-month tour of the Pacific investigating the status of black troops stationed there, and he wrote Walter urging him to see me because he wanted to hire me. Walter saw me on November 22 and approved my being hired as a legal assistant at $1,400 per annum.

Until the fall of 1944 my draft board in East Orange, New Jersey, had not bothered me, but in September, I was told to report. Hastie had given me a letter for just this eventuality in which he set forth my case, which was now pending before the Army Discharge Review Board. In it he depicted Hayes as the villain who had been subjected to military discipline for striking an enlisted man. Then he applied the coup de grâce by describing Hayes as a black who sometimes tried to pass for white. In race relations, New Jersey was akin to a southern state. These middle-aged white men, from backgrounds of deep-seated racial prejudice, were visibly outraged that Hayes should try to be white. I could tell when each of the men got to the passing-for-white part. They would flush red and begin to show anger. They then readily regarded me as being wronged by such an evil man as Hayes must be, and agreed to delay requiring my induction until the Discharge Review Board's decision. The latter hearing had taken place in August and seemed to have gone well.

The draft board cooperated, but the decision of the Discharge Review Board was long in coming. Patton's offensive in Germany had resulted in a great loss of life, and my draft board and others were under pressure to provide more inductees. Finally, in January 1945, with no word from the Discharge Review Board, my draft board decided it could wait no longer and ordered me to report for induction. At induction I was found to have a chronic ear infection, and my induction was deferred for three weeks. A few days after my return home, I was notified that the Discharge Review Board had agreed with Hastie that the administrative proceedings had not been justified, and I was accorded an honorable discharge.

This meant that my draft board had no jurisdiction over me, and I could not be ordered back into the army. Hastie felt I should volunteer to return to the service. The war was not over, and my voluntarily seeking to resume service in the armed forces would clear my record of whatever questions the administrative discharge might raise. Following his advice, I wrote the adjutant general setting forth my credentials and expressing a desire to serve in some capacity in furtherance of the war effort. My application was rejected with a statement of appreciation for the patriotism my application displayed.

Thus ended the military phase of my life. I was not a good soldier, but I could have been better in a less racist environment. I was subjected to humiliation and scarred because of race, but accorded some perks as well. Without the army experience, I might have discounted the impact of race and believed falsely that a black man could rise or fall based solely on his own talents. Nor would I have realized that despite the equivalent of twenty-four years of academic training, I was as vulnerable to destruction through racial discrimination as the poorest and most unlettered black person. Most of all, my time in the army enabled me to focus on a life's mission: to fight to remove the barriers of racial discrimination under which blacks were forced to live. This struggle became central to my professional life for the next quarter century. And in the NAACP as Thurgood Marshall's chief assistant and subsequently as NAACP general counsel I found the means to carry out that mission. Even today, while no longer the central focus of my professional life, the desire to end race discrimination in this country still affects how I think, what I do, and who I am.

*Chapter 4*

# The NAACP Years

**W**hen I joined the NAACP legal staff in November 1944, I came to it in almost total ignorance of its rich history. I had not heard of the *Crisis* and was not aware of how Walter White and Roy Wilkins had risked their lives to amass the facts concerning egregious hardships blacks were systematically being subjected to in parts of the South. I was not even conversant with Thurgood Marshall's accomplishments. This was, in large part, a reflection on my education, not just in the New Jersey public schools, but at Lincoln and Howard as well. The white professors at Lincoln were there to uplift and attempt to civilize their black charges, and had no interest in a rigorous exploration of the black experience in this country. Moreover, their knowledge was probably limited to what I had already been exposed to, which was the accepted version of history. At Howard we did not look back; our task was to gain the tools to deal with the current and existing evil.

The NAACP started its legal staff in 1933, when it received a grant to devise a program to fight discrimination in education. Although the grant was never fully paid, the NAACP decided to proceed anyway. Charles Houston was hired and devised what was to become the genesis of the legal strategy culminating in 1954 in *Brown v. Board*. Houston's strategy was to make segregation too expensive to be sustained. He planned to have qualified blacks apply to the schools of law, medicine, dentistry, journalism—every school of a state university that maintained facilities for whites without providing them for blacks. Under the "separate but equal" doctrine segregation met constitutional requirements if there were substantially equal facilities provided for blacks. Up to Houston's time the equal-facilities part of the "separate but equal" equation had not been tested. He believed that if the states were required to establish separate professional and graduate facilities for blacks where such state facilities were being maintained for whites, the states would find the financial burden too heavy and would abandon segregation with respect to these facilities. Then, with segregation at the university level abandoned, the states would find it difficult to justify its enforcement in other areas, or it would be easier to convince courts to ban the practice.

Thurgood Marshall, Houston's protégé and star pupil from Howard, succeeded Houston as lead counsel for the NAACP in 1938. When I joined the staff, it was housed in a few rooms in the organization's national offices on lower Fifth Avenue in New York. Thurgood had only one full-time assistant, Edward Dudley, a St. John's University Law School graduate. Dudley was a decent lawyer and a very skillful politician. He was to become ambassador to Liberia under President Truman and later a New York family court judge, and would end his career as a New York State Supreme Court justice. Dudley was not interested in research, legal analysis, brief writing, and the concomitant intellectual explorations Thurgood was now going to require. Milton Konvitz, a professor of law from Cornell, could have fulfilled that need, but he was in the office only part-time. On reflection, Konvitz probably had other interests, since I do not recall his participating in any of the strategy sessions involving key cases of the time.

What Thurgood had accomplished by 1945 was simply amazing. He had no law library on the premises, and he relied principally on Bill Hastie and Leon A. Ransom of Howard's faculty to help him get his major brief writing accomplished. Aside from the *Murray v. Maryland* case, he had secured reversals by the United States Supreme Court of several convictions of blacks, on the basis of coerced confessions. Shortly before I came on the scene, he had secured the opening of the Democratic Party primary in the South in the Supreme Court's decision in *Smith v. Allwright*.

At some point in December 1944, some pleading had to be prepared for filing in one of our pending cases. I was the only person with legal knowledge in the office, and the papers had to go out that day. I was reluctant to prepare the papers without being assigned the task. Thurgood's secretary at the time was Anita Riley. She was what was known then as a "tough broad," highly competent, fiercely loyal to Thurgood, yet willing to help one as naive and insecure as I was at the time. She urged me to prepare the document, and with some trepidation I did. I presented the finished papers to Thurgood on his return from lunch for his signature. He read and approved the documents, which were mailed that night, meeting the deadline. That solidified my role as the in-house intellect on whom he relied to see to it that all the legal work that needed to be done was done. I had been admitted to the bar and was now qualified to try cases in court. My work was considered of such high quality by Thurgood and Walter that Walter took the unusual step of writing to members of the board in July 1945 to secure their imme- diate approval of my being upgraded to assistant special counsel at $3,000 per annum.*

As the war drew to a close, the NAACP's legal de- mands were increasing. The mistreatment of black sol- diers had become a major issue, and the escalation of black demands for full citizenship rights stimulated by war accelerated the challenge to Jim Crow. Thurgood was required to travel all over the country encouraging

---

* On July 21, 1945, Bill Hastie wrote Walter approving of my new status and raise in pay. In the letter, which I cherish, as I cherish all the good Bill felt for me, he wrote of my having written the brief and coming to Wash- ington to handle with him the appeal of a court-martial of a Lieutenant Wallace and others. "At my suggestion," Hastie wrote, "he presented prac- tically the entire argument. I offered only a brief summation. He handled the argument with very great ability and on one issue where the Board challenged his argument, he not only stood his ground but, to all outward appearances, persuaded the Board that his position was legally the correct one. His written brief in this case was a very able and mature job."

and counseling NAACP branches on how to pursue the fight against discrimination in their communities. The demand for his presence in the field placed him under enormous pressure in meeting various case filing deadlines. Unless the legal program was to be abandoned, more hands were needed. I became the first of the new hires, and by the end of 1945 Marian Wynn Perry and Franklin Williams had been added, with Constance Motley hired on a part-time basis until her graduation from Columbia, when she became a full-time member of the staff. Marian Perry was an experienced and highly qualified white lawyer, and she was committed to the cause. Franklin Williams was a recent graduate of Fordham Law School. He was a very handsome, well-spoken black man, with the voice, command of language, and presence that could enthrall an audience, and he was extremely ambitious. In September 1949, Jack Greenberg, a recent Columbia University Law School graduate, joined the staff. The staff was rounded out by Annette Peyser, a young white woman, who worked as an assistant to the legal staff, gathering facts and data that might be relevant to our mission.

The NAACP moved from lower Fifth Avenue to 20 West Fortieth Street—the Wendell Willkie Building. I was given a small corner office. The rest of the staff had desks in one large room. Our library problems were solved because we had access to the nearby library of the Association of the Bar of the City of New York, one of the best law libraries in the country. In addition, we were allowed to use the libraries of all the law schools in the city.

As a staff we were determined to be among the best and the brightest. We met twice, then once, a month to discuss any relevant articles in the major law reviews. The pressure of work and travel after a while made that commitment impossible to keep, but Annette Peyser was charged with keeping us informed of all relevant nonlegal developments, publications, ideas, and data that could be used in our briefs or legal arguments. We handled an enormous amount of legal work and worked well together, forging strong personal bonds, in my case with Marian, Franklin (both of whom are now deceased), and Connie.

In the immediate postwar years, this small but highly talented staff handled a broad range of cases challenging segregation and discrimination. From 1945 through 1947 our caseload included Democratic Party primary cases in South Carolina and Alabama to implement the 1944 *Smith v. Allwright* ruling, and numerous transportation cases challenging segregated seating and dining car service on interstate railroads. I had begun to take a number of these cases before the Interstate Commerce Commission. *Sweatt v. Painter,* seeking Heman Sweatt's admission to the University of Texas, was on our calendar, along with *Sipuel v. University of Oklahoma* and two cases against the University of Louisiana. We also defended some twenty-seven blacks who had been indicted for various crimes in connection with the 1946 race riot in Columbia, Tennessee. We filed a brief amicus curiae in the Ohio State Supreme Court defending the constitutionality of the recently enacted Ohio Civil Rights Statute. Several cases attacking the validity of racial restrictive covenants were begun. We succeeded in having the murder conviction of one Willie Carter overturned and a new trial ordered in Mississippi, and we brought several employment discrimination cases before the New York State Commission Against Discrimination.

In 1946, Thurgood and Bill Hastie argued the NAACP's first transportation case before the Supreme Court. Irene Morgan, who was traveling from Gloucester County, Virginia, to Baltimore, refused to move to the back of the bus as required by Virginia law, claiming that the law did not apply to her because she was an interstate passenger. As part of this case, Virginia attorney Spottswood Robinson and I researched the various state laws as to who was officially a black, and found a crazy quilt of varying requirements—from one drop of black blood in one state to a different quality in the next and a third formula in the third state. Each of the eleven Confederate states had its own definition. We presented this as evidence that the requirement that the bus carrier implement these laws placed an unconstitutional burden on commerce. In the end, the Supreme Court voted 7–1 to overturn segregation on interstate buses.

Franklin Williams and I were sitting together in the Supreme Court listening to Thurgood and Hastie argue *Morgan v. Virginia*. I was in awe. Frank said, "I could do as well," and he believed it. To me, what I had just witnessed—a cogent, confident articulation of legal principles by two black lawyers before judges of the highest court in the country who seemed persuaded that the argument had merit—mirrored my highest aspirations. I wanted to develop into the kind of lawyer I had just seen.

I worried that I might never be a good or successful lawyer. I did not have a good speaking voice, which I believed at the time was essential for courtroom success. I was also extremely shy, particularly in a public setting. I realized that in order to emulate what I had just witnessed, I had to learn my craft thoroughly and become a finished lawyer. When I took a case to court I had to be thoroughly conversant with every factual detail involved and have at my fingertips every aspect of the law applicable to the case being presented.

I did not have the desire or personality to be a civil rights leader who could stir the masses to action, but I could aim to become one of the best civil rights lawyers in the country—the kind that has come to be classified as a technocrat. I am reasonably confident that I achieved that objective. Frank Williams, in contrast, wanted to be a civil rights leader, which immediately put him on a collision course with Thurgood and Roy Wilkins, but surprisingly enough, Walter White and he got along well together.

During 1946, the legal campaign to secure equal educational opportunity for blacks accelerated. We had a major conference in Atlanta, Georgia, on April 27–28, 1946, with the lawyers with whom we worked to determine the most effective litigation strategy to advance the struggle for quality education from grade school to professional school. Later in the year I wrote what was to be the first draft of the ultimate brief challenging school segregation directly as a violation of the Fourteenth Amendment.

The Atlanta conference brought together the leading civil rights lawyers of the day. They included: Leon A.

Ransom, a brilliant legal scholar and Charles Houston disciple, who taught at Howard University Law School; Oliver Hill; and Spottswood Robinson, who along with Martin A. Martin were partners in a law firm in Richmond, Virginia. All three were Howard University Law graduates. Hill and Martin were classmates of Thurgood's. Robinson was a year ahead of me and graduated with the highest grade point average ever achieved at the school. They were the first of the local lawyers we could rely on to draft proper pleadings; the rest of this work had to be done in our New York office. Also attending was Arthur D. Shores of Birmingham, Alabama, who refused to be intimidated by city or state officials and filed equal rights litigation despite threats. A.P. Tureaud of New Orleans was another local practitioner on whom we could rely to actively instigate and pursue equal rights litigation, as was J.R. Booker of Little Rock, Arkansas. A.T. Walden of Atlanta was probably one of the oldest black lawyers in the country. He was past his prime and had to look to us to do all the work, but he stood by us in court and made clear that he was fully involved in the litigation being pursued. He secured access to the premises where the two-day meeting was held. In addition, lawyers from Nashville, Tennessee; South Carolina; Washington, D.C.; and Florida were in attendance. Thurgood chaired the conference, and I was given the task of making a digest of the proceedings.

The conference began with a survey of the educational profile of each state beginning at the university level. The various legal approaches—injunction, mandamus, state or federal—were discussed. The consensus was that a state court remedy was preferred. We considered a broad range of questions and strategies. Should we initiate proceedings for admission to the white facility when nothing equivalent was available for blacks? How would we get the judges to use specific measurements in an equal-facility equation? What was the best strategy for getting a judge to require equal bus facilities for black children? Oliver Hill had taken a group of black children to the bus pickup for white children, insisting they be allowed on the bus, which resulted in a bus being made available for black children. That tactic did not usually work, however.

It was agreed that cases for law school admission in Oklahoma and Tennessee should be vigorously pursued, litigation for such admission in Louisiana and South Carolina would be filed immediately, and we should explore the possibility of litigation for law school admission in Texas. Arthur Shores and I reported that we might have a candidate for law school admission to the University of Alabama, but there were no cases in sight yet in Florida or Virginia. We had a number of possible cases for elementary and secondary school equalization litigation in Virginia, Maryland, and Florida, and possible vocational school litigation in Arkansas, Alabama, and Washington, D.C.

This was my first such conference. It was a very stimulating exercise, sitting around a table with other black men (this was before Constance Motley joined us) exchanging views about what should and could be done with our legal talent to better the lot of black children. Beginning in 1948, after a brief leave of absence to work with the American Veterans Committee, I organized all such conferences, selected the participants, chose the topics to be discussed, and chaired the discussions. Most of the subsequent meetings had far more intellectual heft than the meeting in 1946. But while all these conferences were exhilarating, they never matched the thrill of my first exposure.

After arguing the *Morgan* case, Thurgood contracted a respiratory infection and had to spend five or six weeks away from the office recuperating. I was left in charge of the staff. During his absence school officials in Southern California began to enroll Mexican children in a separate school in the Westminster School District, on the grounds that they would learn English more quickly. While there was evidence of the children being short-changed in books, equipment, and teaching personnel, the federal judge before whom the case was tried ruled that segregation per se was a denial of equal educational opportunities, an exciting development for civil rights lawyers.

With the case pending before the Ninth Circuit, I decided to file a brief amicus curiae for the NAACP in support of the judge's position that segregation in and of itself was unconstitutional. In the course of my research I came across a brief of Charles Sumner, later one of the leaders of the Radical Republicans who led the drive for enactment of the Thirteenth, Fourteenth, and Fifteenth Amendments to the Constitution and various civil rights laws seeking to ensure equal citizenship for the newly freed slaves and to insulate them from all the vestiges of slavery. The 1849 case *Roberts v. City of Boston* involved segregation of black children in Boston's public schools.

What was fascinating was that Sumner's argument made some five score years earlier was so timely and pertinent to the present. I quoted extensively from the brief in urging the Ninth Circuit to hold with the trial judge that segregation itself was illegal. The brief was really my baby. Loren Miller, a member of our National Legal Committee and a major intellect, was the only person with a real opportunity to modify what I had written, but he liked what was presented to him. I made certain that Thurgood had the opportunity to study the brief and suggest changes before it was filed, but he let it go as written.

The Ninth Circuit resisted our attempt to have them forecast *Brown* and affirmed on equal facilities grounds. The brief in *Mendez v. Westminster School District* was an initial trial run of what was to come. While we had not yet become involved in attacking grade- and secondary-school segregation, we knew that soon that issue had to be faced. Before long, Thurgood returned to the office restored to good health.

In the spring of 1946, I met Gloria Spencer through Ernest Rice, a mutual friend. He and Gloria had been dating, but I moved right in. A graduate of Hunter College, Gloria lived in Harlem and worked as a social worker. She was a vivacious and sophisticated brown-skinned woman. With her I made my first forays into Harlem, where we enjoyed the club scene and the nightlife. It was a whirlwind romance. When I brought a woman home to meet my mother and sisters in the past, their comment would invariably be "She's nice, but . . ." But when I brought Gloria to meet them, I announced that she and I were going to be married, and that was that. But it was a perfect fit. They were devoted to her; my mother really loved her. In fact, Gloria could do no wrong in their eyes. If there was a problem, then clearly I was at fault.

We married on December 6, 1946. After spending a night at the Taft Hotel in New York we left for Birmingham, Alabama, and New Orleans. I was to try my first case in Montgomery, Alabama, a voting rights case coming out of Macon County, Alabama. Then we would continue on to New Orleans for a belated honeymoon of about ten days. Gloria took it all in stride. The trip was her first to the South. She was a very personable young woman with impeccable good manners, so the southern men and women took to her right away.

Arthur Shores, the local NAACP attorney in Birmingham, met us at the airport. He was one of those heroic black lawyers of the South who attacked discrimination in the courts despite being under constant threat of violence to himself and his family. When he asked me to open the glove compartment of the car, I saw he kept a gun there and knew this was serious business. We stayed at his home for the several days we were there. Mrs. Shores was a very soft-spoken woman. They had two young girls. Arthur had them on a shooting range regularly, making certain they knew how to handle a gun. Arthur said if racists came after him, he and his family would not be the only ones hurt.

I was nervous to say the least trying my first case with my wife in the audience, but she and Arthur congratulated me on my performance. The case, *Mitchell v. Wright*, was brought by the Tuskegee Civic Association (TCA) and challenged the board of registrars for unfairly rejecting the applications of twenty-five blacks who had attempted to register. William Mitchell, an employee at the Veterans Hospital in Tuskegee, was the plaintiff. We lost the case at the trial level and appealed it to the Fifth Circuit Court of Appeals. Before the case could be heard, the authorities "discovered" that the board of registrars had already registered Mitchell, thus ending the suit. The TCA, however, pressed ahead, and in 1960 I would represent its leader, Charles Gomillion, in arguably the most important voting rights case to reach the Supreme Court up to that time.

We had a good time in Birmingham, the Shores and their friends seeing to it that we enjoyed the warmth and plentitude of southern hospitality. We were given a few days to enjoy ourselves in New Orleans, and then the NAACP people took over our social life. It was a good experience for us both. Gloria was a native New Yorker whose social life had been chiefly in integrated circles in the city. She had had no exposure to black social life in the South. After ten days in New Orleans, she returned to New York while I remained in New Orleans a few days longer to prepare for and argue an appeal in one of our Democratic Party primary cases before the United States Court of Appeals for the Fifth Circuit. The appellate argument went well. I knew the law and the facts and was not fazed or intimidated by the questions put to me. I returned to New York with two career milestones accomplished: I had my first trial and first appellate argument.

In New York I was faced with the pressing personal problem of finding decent affordable housing—a problem that returning veterans and the young at the beginning of marriage and career face. The Metropolitan Life Insurance Company had built Stuyvesant Town, a huge complex of efficiency to three-bedroom apartments on the Lower East Side of Manhattan. It was the largest housing complex yet erected in the city. The land was made available through state condemnation proceeding, and as a further inducement to build the project and to keep the rents at reasonable levels, Metropolitan was granted tax abatements for years and various government subsidies. Despite federal, state, and city involvement, Metropolitan refused to allow blacks to live there.

In an apparent effort to avoid a lawsuit and to quiet criticism that the company was guilty of racial discrimination, Metropolitan built Riverton, a housing project in Harlem for blacks, on Fifth Avenue from East 135th to 137th streets. The apartments were chiefly efficiency, one-, and two-bedroom units, with one three-bedroom apartment in each building. The rooms were smaller than those in Stuyvesant Town, but the project was well maintained and the rents were affordable. Riverton housed a large segment of the up-and-coming black middle class— doctors; lawyers; college professors and public school teachers; city, state, and federal officials; and middle-level employees. Constance and Joel Motley, Franklin and Shirley Williams, and Gloria and I lived there, and our children were born while we were there. Most of us stayed at Riverton for ten or more years before moving on to more spacious housing in the city or deserting the city entirely for suburban life.

Looking back on it now, it seems strange that even with the state's antidiscrimination law in place, Metropol-

itan could practice such blatant discrimination and sponsor racial segregation with impunity. I was housed at
Riverton before and after the *Brown* proceedings, completely engaged body and soul in an all-out effort to eliminate racial discrimination from America. Yet it never
occurred to me that I should refuse to live at Riverton in
space made available by a racist landholder. This is a
dilemma most urban blacks faced. Decent affordable
housing was a dire immediate need, and that need was
met only within the strictures of segregation—one could
reject either the segregation or the housing.

Toward the closing days of 1946, the U.S. Senate appointed a special committee to investigate the Mississippi
Democratic primary campaign of Senator Theodore G.
Bilbo. At a public hearing in Jackson, Mississippi, several
qualified black electors testified about their attempts to
register and vote in the face of vocal threats from Bilbo
himself and actual violence from his henchmen. On the
basis of that testimony we submitted a formal brief on
January 1, 1947, and cited several precedents providing
the legal basis for the Senate to refuse to seat Bilbo because of his attempts to disenfranchise black voters of
Mississippi. In January 1947, when Bilbo presented himself at the door of the Senate to take his seat, he was asked
to step aside. Before action on his case could be completed, Bilbo became ill and died.

In 1947 we were engaged, as usual, in a wide range of
legal activity. We still had to bring cases to secure implementation of *Smith v. Allwright* to open the Democratic
Party primary to black voters. We still had to litigate to
enable blacks to register and vote in much of the South

despite the Fifteenth Amendment guarantee of that right. The most significant case in this category was one in South Carolina before Judge J. Waities Waring. Judge Waring was the first of the maverick southern judges who began issuing decisions enforcing the Fourteenth and Fifteenth Amendment strictures on behalf of black complainants. He was a member of an old-line South Carolina family, but his decisions were at war with the fervently held beliefs of his peers, and for that he was ostracized.

Our attack on segregation at the law school and graduate school level had intensified. The case of Ada Lois Sipuel seeking admission to the University of Oklahoma Law School was accepted for argument before the United States Supreme Court in November 1947. We made a major attack on segregation in the retrial of Heman Sweatt's effort to secure admission to the University of Texas Law School. In response to Sweatt's initial challenge, the district court ruled that the state must either admit him or establish a law school for black students. The Texas state legislature appropriated funds for a new law school to be housed temporarily in the basement of an office building in downtown Austin. Sweatt went back to court, and Thurgood handled the retrial with W.J. Durham and several other Texas attorneys. At the trial Thurgood put on a stellar group of experts in law and social science: Dr. Earl Harrison of the University of Pennsylvania Law School; Dr. Malcolm Sharp of the University of Chicago Law School; Dr. Charles Thompson, dean of the School of Education at Howard University; and Dr. Robert Redfield, head of the Department of

Anthropology at the University of Chicago. Their testimony and the evidence presented offered a powerful challenge to segregation per se as illegal. The court, however, ruled against Sweatt, and the case was taken up on appeal. A case was pending on our calendar for admission to the medical school of Louisiana State University as well, but nothing ever came of it.

During this time, my civil rights work took a slight detour. The American Veterans Committee (AVC) had recently been formed to meet the needs of World War II veterans. One of the primary desires of the organizers was that the membership and power structure would be racially mixed. Friends urged Frank Williams and me to attend the first convention of the group, scheduled for the summer of 1947 in Des Moines, Iowa. A national headquarters was set up in Washington, D.C., and I was asked to join the staff as director of veterans affairs. I asked for and secured permission for a year's leave of absence from the NAACP beginning October 1, 1947.

John, my first child, was born in July 1947. In October 1947 I went to Washington alone. I had arranged to stay with Beth and Frank Reeves, a couple I had become close to in my days at Howard Law School. Beth was and still is a very beautiful and intellectually gifted woman. She has a doctorate in speech therapy. Frank was a graduate of Howard Law School, taught at the school, and was very active in our legal work. He performed the role of big brother, helping me solve legal problems and defusing some awkward social situations. Frank had a serious weight problem, which he was not able to correct. This apparently weakened his heart, and he died young, leaving a void in my life that was never filled.

Finding affordable housing for my family proved more difficult than I had thought, and I spent about three months in the Reeveses' apartment before I was able to bring Gloria and John to Washington in January 1948.

The AVC assignment was a disappointment. I met some interesting people, some of whom would gain national leadership stature. The organization, unfortunately, was so torn by ideological strife that the hoped-for effective vehicle of national influence and power to meet the needs of the new veterans was never realized. It soon became evident that I would resign before being a year in the position.

Adding to my restlessness and making more urgent the need to return to New York was the fact that Gloria could not adjust to Washington. We had a wide circle of friends whose company Gloria very much enjoyed. In our trip to Birmingham and New Orleans, at Riverton, and now in Washington, Gloria was meeting and socializing with large numbers of well-educated black men and women to whom she had not been exposed before. She enjoyed that and made lasting friendships. But she had never before had to face segregation head-on, and having to live under such restrictions in the nation's capital was very depressing. She lost a great deal of weight and was clearly unhappy.

Thurgood and I were together in Washington in May 1948. We did not talk about my return to New York, but in a letter dated May 13, 1948, he wrote that he had planned to talk to me about coming back to my old job when he saw me the previous week but had failed to get to it. He had heard that I planned to return in the early fall and added, "I am sure you know, but I want you to have it officially, that we will be more than happy to have you back. We most certainly need you—the sooner, the better." He asked me to confirm my plans to return in a personal letter, letting him know when I wished to report to work. I took up my NAACP chores again in the early fall of 1948. When I returned, Thurgood went out of his way to make clear my position as his chief deputy.

As second in command, I was faced with an immediate and pressing personnel problem. During his tenure as principal NAACP lawyer no one other than Thurgood had argued a case in the Supreme Court, but the staff had grown, as had the number of cases on our calendar that we hoped the Court would agree to hear. It was clear that the "Thurgood-only" rule could not long survive. At this time Frank Williams had been working on the case of a black defendant from Indiana convicted and sentenced to death. Frank had filed the petition for writ of certiorari seeking review by the high court, and the petition had been granted. He had also written the brief on the merits. The case was set for argument in a matter of weeks, but no word had come from Thurgood on whether Frank would be allowed to make the Supreme Court argument; to say that Frank was frantic is an understatement.

There was no question in my mind that Frank, who had done all the work necessary to get the case before the Court as well as the brief on the merits, which we had approved as meeting staff standards, should be permitted to make the Supreme Court argument. As staff chief deputy it was clear that it was my responsibility to try to persuade Thurgood to give Frank this earned opportunity. I found Thurgood alone in his office one afternoon and tried to persuade him to let Frank make the argument. Thurgood's first response was that Frank should not be allowed to make a Supreme Court argument before I did. That was easy to counter. I told him my time would come. Frank had just earned the right before me, and it should be given to him.

A basic reason for Thurgood's resistance was that he did not like or trust Frank. Frank had an aura of ruthless ambition, but he also had those qualities of civil rights leadership that could make the two of them rivals. As a black man Frank had had to fight for every success he had achieved. Thurgood knew that Frank had earned the right to argue the case, and my coming to him on Frank's behalf put him on the defensive. Before giving the okay, however, he decided to get Bill Hastie's reaction. Hastie told him that for the sake of staff morale he had to allow Frank to argue the case before the Supreme Court. When Thurgood concluded his conversation with Hastie, he told me to tell Frank to prepare for the argument. Thurgood would probably have reached this conclusion without my intervention, since there was no one other than Frank prepared to take on the assignment.

The case was *Watts v. Indiana*. Frank made a superb presentation and secured a reversal by a unanimous Court. He was given concrete evidence that Justice Felix Frankfurter thought highly of his presentation. William Coleman, who later became involved with us during the preparation of the Supreme Court brief and argument in the *Brown* case and still later was secretary of transportation, was one of Justice Frankfurter's law clerks at the time. I suppose because both Coleman and Frank were black, Justice Frankfurter sent Coleman a note telling him to come to the courtroom to hear Frank's fine argument. Coleman gave Frank the note, which Frank thereafter proudly displayed among his most treasured mementos.

Throughout my NAACP career each member of the legal staff had to work simultaneously on a wide variety of matters. We were a small operation trying to use the law to revolutionize race relations by seeking to have the Thirteenth, Fourteenth, and Fifteenth Amendments given their intended effect. Racial discrimination was not only operative in all aspects of American life but generally accepted as the appropriate norm. Most white Americans believed that blacks did not and could not be the equal of whites and that second-class status was where we belonged. The staff was able to make and follow a planned program, particularly in education, but sometimes organizational imperatives caused us to pursue issues that on our own we might have deferred for a while. Fortunately, the balance between pursuing a planned program and taking on an issue ad hoc never got out of hand, because the local and national leaderships of the NAACP were as one with the planned program, and pursuing it was usually given priority.

Upon my return to the office in 1948, I began work on a case seeking equal salaries for black and white teachers in Jackson, Mississippi. The lead plaintiff was Gladys Noel Bates, a science teacher at the Smith Robinson

School in Jackson. Mrs. Bates had put her neck on the block in 1946 by making a formal complaint about being paid less than white teachers. As a result she had been fired. Her husband had lost his job as well, and while now both were employed, their current positions paid far less than they had been paid previously. The Bates family was suffering financially. The black teachers in the state had asked for our help, but had not given Mrs. Bates or her family any financial help. When I resumed working on the case, I succeeded in having the Black Teachers Association provide a stipend for Mrs. Bates while the case proceeded through the courts. With Mrs. Bates no longer being employed in the system, R. Jesse Brown joined the lawsuit as an intervener.

In 1949, Constance Motley and I tried the case in the federal court in Jackson, Mississippi. At the time of the lawsuit, fifty of the fifty-three white teachers in the system were paid more than all but one of the fifty black teachers. The principal of the white high school received a salary of $6,300 as opposed to $3,000 for the black high school principal. White elementary-school teachers were paid $4,000 to $4,300 a year, but the highest salary for any black elementary-school teacher was $2,400. We lost the case in the trial court and on appeal on the grounds that we had not exhausted administrative remedies, and the Supreme Court refused review. We were preparing another case, but the state legislature, apparently seeing a losing fight, equalized the salaries early in the 1950s.

The case was more or less legally routine and deserves mention here only because blacks in Mississippi had never seen black lawyers stand up to white officials and have them squirming on the witness stand under relentless, sometimes patient, sometimes withering cross-examination. This was Constance Motley's initiation—her first trial. Neither blacks nor whites had seen a black woman lawyer before. Blacks crowded the courtroom, and the trial became public theater. They took vicarious pride in our performances in court and reenacted scenes from the trial in barbershops and beauty parlors, at parties, in backyards, wherever groups gathered. We provided hope that their exploitation, hurt, and humiliation because of being black might be eliminated someday. I also believe we instilled in some boys and girls the desire to study law. Today a black woman lawyer is no longer uncommon in Mississippi, and many black lawyers of both sexes now practicing in the state are capable of performing in a courtroom as well, if not better, than we did before those admiring black onlookers in 1949.

On January 17, 1949, my participation commenced in another major case, whose reverberations I feel to this day. The case involved representing three black soldiers charged with raping a white civilian. I had received a letter that day signed by Chaplain E.E. Grimmett of the headquarters of the 374th Troop Carrier Wing, stationed on Guam, stating that he believed Calvin and Herman Dennis and Robert Burns, charged with the rape and murder of Ruth Farnsworth, were innocent and that Calvin and Herman Dennis had been terrorized into signing confessions. He asked for our help, and said that funds were being raised and he could guarantee our expenses. On January 27, 1949, I responded to the chaplain by letter and cablegram. He was advised of the great expense involved in travel and was asked to give us some idea of how much money would be available so that we could determine whether to secure a private attorney or assign one of our staff to handle the matter. However, we received a subsequent letter from the chaplain telling us that no definite amount of money could be guaranteed, as the commanding general had stymied their fund-raising efforts.

The three soldiers were returned to military jurisdiction, and a field-grade investigation was launched to determine whether the men would proceed by court-martial. If a court-martial was ordered, the men would be represented by qualified attorneys and the military authorities would see to it that the men's rights under the Constitution and Articles of War were fully protected. Although President Truman had ordered the integration of the armed forces, they were still in the grip of bias and the attitude of an officer corps holding on to and acting upon racial prejudice. The accused were black; the victim, white. Tension was high. Blacks were convinced the men were innocent and being railroaded. Whites on the base were certain of the men's guilt.

After the initial exchange of letters nothing further was heard from Guam until April 4, 1949, when the chaplain sent a cablegram advising that the court-martial proceedings were scheduled to commence on April 8, 1949, and that competent counsel had been selected to defend the men, and suggesting that we send a correspondent. We did nothing further. Then in June 1949 we began receiving a number of letters asking that we represent these men on appeal. The chaplain was informed that we could represent the men only if the men asked us to. In due course such requests were made. Thereupon, we asked for and received permission to intervene on the men's behalf in seeking a new trial or an opportunity, before confirmation of the sentences (each man had a separate court-martial), to review the records and make formal appearances before the review boards. Permission to appear before the review boards was granted, and such appearances were set for October 3, 1949, in Washington.

I went to Washington a few days early to talk to former lieutenant colonel Edward Fenwick Daly, a black officer stationed on Guam at the time the three men were embroiled in this controversy, but now retired from the armed services and practicing law in Washington. He had been one of the officers who had participated in the investigation of the charges leveled against these men. Mary Louise Hill, Daly's secretary in Guam, was also his secretary in Washington.

The two told me a gruesome tale of what had happened to the three men. Herman Dennis was single, twenty years of age, and now on his second tour of duty as an ammunition handler. Calvin Dennis (no relation) was twenty-seven years old and was serving his second term of enlistment. He was a truck driver and had been on duty in Guam since 1948. Staff Sergeant Robert W. Burns was thirty-two years old and single; during World War II he had served in the army ground forces in the Pacific and been awarded the Purple Heart, the Bronze Star, and the Philippine Liberation Ribbon. He had enlisted in the air force in January 1948 and had come to Guam in June 1948, assigned as a mess sergeant.

On December 11, 1948, Ruth Farnsworth, a white civilian working on Guam, was found missing under circumstances that led to the belief that a crime had been committed. On December 13, 1948, she was found in a wooded area near her place of employment in a critical condition. Medical examination indicated that she had been beaten and raped. She was taken to the hospital but died the next day without ever recovering consciousness. An investigation by Guam authorities found no suspects.

On January 7, 1949, a smock identified as belonging to the victim was found by Guam police authorities under the driver's seat of a truck that had been dispatched to Calvin Dennis on December 11. A number of black soldiers were picked up and questioned. The police centered their investigation on Calvin and Herman Dennis and Burns. The men were picked up and turned over to the civilian government of Guam on January 7, 1949. They were immediately placed in solitary confinement, and were permitted no mail and no access to visitors or other outside communication, except the chaplain and defense counsel—but since they did not have counsel, the latter was of little avail. According to the men, they were never advised of their rights, were subjected to continuous questioning, and were threatened, intimidated, and beaten until Calvin and Herman signed statements confessing the crime and implicating Burns. No official charges were leveled against them until January 17, 1949, however, when they were brought before a magistrate and charged with the crime. They were still held in jail under the authority of the Guam civil government until roughly January 30, and during the entire period of their being in the custody of Guam authorities, the only people allowed access to them were a chaplain, the police, and military authorities.

Daly said that he informed the command headquarters that the Guam government had no jurisdiction over the men, since this would be a denial of the airmen's constitutional rights in view of the agreement between the United States and the government of Guam concerning procedures to be followed in civilian cases. The air force then took custody of the men and carried out its own investigation, which resulted in court-martial proceedings being instituted.

The men's confessions had been obtained without their being advised of their rights against self-incrimination under the Fifth Amendment and the Twenty-fourth Article of War. According to Daly, the man prosecuting the court-martial charges knew the men had not been warned of their rights. The official who took Calvin's and Herman's confessions at first said the men had not been advised of their rights, but changed his testimony on the witness stand and said they had been so advised.

Daly accused the official who obtained the evidence introduced at each court-martial (the three men had separate trials) of being overzealous because of a setback in his career. His suspicions were rooted in the blatant evidence of witness tampering prior to the trials. Several of the witnesses in the case had come to Daly asking him to explain what perjury meant. These men told Daly that the prosecutor had advised them that if they testified at trial to what they believed was true and were convinced happened, they would be tried for perjury. A Sergeant Wright had consulted the trial judge advocate, Lieutenant Colonel Magnese, who had referred him to Daly. Magnese had then called Daly and told him to do everything possible to get Sergeant Wright to testify contrary to his convictions.

Defense counsel were given only one day to prepare. In each of the three separate court-martial trials, the defense took only one hour to present a case in the men's defense.

Apart from the flawed confessions there was nothing of substance to sustain the convictions. A witness testified to seeing the accused, or someone looking like Herman Dennis and another man, close to the scene of the crime either before or after the event. On cross-examination, however, he admitted testifying at the investigation that the men appeared to be Filipino soldiers. There was testimony about bloodstains on the clothing of the accused that was analyzed as human, but Burns explained that the blood on his clothing resulted from his conducting meat-cutting classes. Hair samples found on the accused's clothing was analyzed as looking like the hair from a Caucasian and from persons of Negroid ethnicity, but that alone was insufficient to sustain convictions warranting a life sentence or the death penalty.

At the Burns court-martial, Calvin Dennis—who signed four confessions, each different from the other— testified, implicating Burns. Later, Dennis recanted, stating in an affidavit that he had committed perjury on the promise of the trial judge advocate of a lesser sentence, and because of physical coercion by the prosecutor, threats by investigators "to pin murder and rape and kid-napping on me," and by offers of part of a $4,000 reward if he implicated Burns.

My efforts to secure a new trial for these soldiers con-tinued as the fight against school segregation intensified.

In 1948, the *Sipuel* case culminated with a Supreme Court ruling that allowed Oklahoma to satisfy the "equal pro-tection" requirement of the Fourteenth Amendment by offering a makeshift law school for Ada Sipuel "and oth-ers similarly situated" in a roped-off section of the state capitol. That August we took another graduate school case that helped broaden our challenge to the fiction of separate but equal. George McLaurin applied for admis-sion to the graduate program in education at the Univer-sity of Oklahoma and was rejected. The NAACP took McLaurin's case before a special three-judge federal dis-trict court, which ruled that the state was required "to provide the plaintiff with the education he seeks as soon as it does for applicants of any other group." Oklahoma complied by admitting McLaurin to the University of Oklahoma, but the legislature held that instruction must be given on a segregated basis. McLaurin was, in effect, set apart from the rest of the student body through a vari-ety of makeshift arrangements. We immediately appealed the *McLaurin v. Oklahoma State Regent* case to the U.S. Supreme Court.

In June 1949 we met in New York with forty-three lawyers and fourteen NAACP branch and state confer-ence presidents from twenty-two states and the District of Columbia to discuss and agree upon legal strategy to pursue in college, graduate school, professional school, and transportation cases. While all legal conferences were called in Thurgood's name, it was my responsibility until 1956 to set the agenda and decide whom to invite, subject to Thurgood's approval, which was never withheld. We agreed that we should attack segregation as being per se unconstitutional, and simultaneously establish the physical disparities between white and black educational facilities.

On November 14, 1949, after the Court had set down *McLaurin v. Oklahoma State Regent, Sweatt v. Painter,* and *Henderson v. U.S.* for argument in the spring of 1950, I issued a memorandum to the staff calling for research in various topics in preparation for writing the *McLaurin* and *Sweatt* briefs. (*Henderson* challenged segregation on railroad dining cars, a practice that had the sanction of the Interstate Commerce Commission; it was not our case.) Persons assigned specific topics were to thoroughly support their conclusions with cases, articles, and other material and be prepared to defend whatever conclusions they reached. My assignment was to establish that governmental racial classifications were unreasonable and without relationship to the subject matter, and therefore void under the Fourteenth Amendment. *Plessy v. Ferguson,* I argued, was wrongly decided because discrimination was inevitable under the separate but equal doctrine, and its intent was to maintain blacks in an inferior color caste status. There were unreasonable inconsistencies, that is, in the various statements of the formula, which invited litigation.

Thurgood and I developed the argument that *McLaurin* showed no need for segregation in terms of public order, but that its real purpose was to maintain the subordination of blacks in an inferior caste status. Thurgood was also to show disparities between the law school established for *Sweatt* and that of the University of Texas, and that where segregation has been discontinued in graduate and professional schools, the experiment has worked: that no problems of public disorder had occurred, and both the state and the individual benefited.

We had a group of Columbia University law students of Professor Walter Gelhorn doing volunteer work. I asked them to tell us the status of the law on segregation in education at the time the Fourteenth Amendment was passed, anticipating the question that the Supreme Court would raise in 1953. The legislative history and the inquiry concerning the status of the law were inconclusive.

We were severely criticized by some blacks and segments of the black press for taking the *McLaurin* case to the Supreme Court. The argument of our critics was that there was too great a risk that the Court would rule against us, causing a devastating reversal of the gains made in the effort to outlaw segregation. The struggle for equality for blacks was too important for it to be put at such risk. The reason for our critics' concern was that *McLaurin* fulfilled the separate but equal doctrine's requirements. We could not argue that the physical facilities or quality of the teaching personnel or the teaching McLaurin received was not on par with that of the white students. McLaurin was admitted to the University of Oklahoma, not assigned to a separate school for blacks.

He attended the same classes as his fellow white students, was instructed by the same professors, and had to study out of the same texts. He was assigned to sit in a special seat in the classroom, to a special table in the library, and to a special chair in the cafeteria. Our critics felt this would be received by the Supreme Court as too insubstantial a racial burden to warrant constitutional prohibition. Marjorie McKenzie, a columnist for the *Pittsburgh Courier*, an influential black newspaper of national reach, made the critics' case most forcibly.

Thurgood was sufficiently concerned about the criticism that he arranged to bring together those favoring our handling of *McLaurin* to a conference at Howard University, to have persons of prominence and influence make and support our argument for going forward with the case. One of the speakers was W.E.B. DuBois, whom I had never heard speak before. His concern was the economic exploitation of black people. He gave a list of concrete areas and ways in which blacks were being exploited, and ended with the admonition "Know the facts and the facts will set you free." It was an impressive speech and for me an overwhelming experience hearing for the first time this great intellect sharing his views with an audience. I do not remember Dr. DuBois saying anything in support of our position in the *McLaurin* case, but he knew the purpose of the conference and joined it. That was enough for us to claim him as favoring our pushing ahead with the case.

Calling the Howard University conference was evidence of Thurgood's political and public relations skills. He was going to proceed with the case without regard to his critics, but he regarded it as politic not to allow his critics to have the field to themselves in voicing their views. The conference was designed not only as a challenge to Marjorie McKenzie and the others clamoring for abandonment of the case, but to put them on the defensive regarding their position—as compared to the views of prominent black lawyers, educators, clergymen, and social scientists who supported our position. The criticism did not abate until the Supreme Court published its opinion, holding that the university's treatment of McLaurin infringed on his right to equal educational opportunity.

Being proved wrong, however, did not silence Ms. McKenzie. When she learned of our attack on segregation per se in our 1951 appeal to the United States Supreme Court from the three-judge court decisions in the school segregation cases in South Carolina (*Briggs v. Elliott*) and Topeka, Kansas (*Brown v. Board of Education*), she was out in full force again with a column on the first page of the *Pittsburgh Courier*. She was a lawyer and wrote with a clear, cogent style. She had as an audience those in the black community who felt we might be moving too fast as well as those who feared that elimination of segregation would mean a loss of the security that the system afforded them.

I was supposed to argue the *Sweatt* case before the high court. I wrote the brief with Jack Greenberg's assistance. Thurgood had assigned the writing of the *McLaurin* brief to himself. At the last minute, however, I had to write the *McLaurin* brief as well. Thurgood also had a change of heart about the argument so that *McLaurin*, not *Sweatt*, became my assignment—my first appearance before the Supreme Court.

I was on cloud nine, my dream fulfilled. Every American lawyer hopes to have a case before the Supreme Court. When that hope is realized, however, the exhilaration is tempered by anxiety. Those were certainly my feelings. I went to Washington about a week before the argument was scheduled to take place, but I had to leave Washington for Minneapolis immediately prior to the argument to fulfill a prior commitment. Although May, it snowed in Minneapolis and was very cold. When I returned to Washington the day before I was to appear before the Court, I was fighting a cold and hoarseness.

Amos Hall, the local lawyer from Tulsa whose case it was, was to share the argument with me. Amos wanted merely to make a perfunctory appearance, leaving the essence of the presentation to me. I was very nervous, as I usually am initially before an audience, and very worried that nervousness might overwhelm me. At that time each side was given an hour to present its case. *McLaurin* was the last case to be called that day, at 4:05 P.M. The Court recessed at 4:30 P.M. Amos took only ten minutes, leaving me fifteen minutes before the recess. I conquered my nerves, and because the Court was tired and looking forward to the recess, I was allowed to speak without interruption until the Court adjourned for the day.

Thurgood, our staff, and all the lawyers supporting us then convened in the lawyers' lounge in the Supreme Court building with me to critique my performance. I was uniformly praised for the argument. My confidence was given such a boost that when I began the argument the next day, I was completely at ease, to the point of arrogance. The questions came fast and furious, but I was able to deal with all of them with composure and assurance.

I have seen lawyers come apart in first-time appearances before the Supreme Court and realize that with my insecurity in public speaking, it could easily have happened to me. What saved me was the fortuity of beginning my argument at the end of the day. With about half an hour to put me on the griddle the next day, the Court allowed me precious time to gain needed confidence. Although I was usually nervous at the start of each of the succeeding appearances before the Court, that disappeared as the argument progressed, and I was always so fully conversant with the facts and relevant law that I was able to answer satisfactorily all inquiries. With each argument my confidence grew that I could meet every challenge from the Court. Eventually, I became confident of possessing sufficient skill to hold my own in any appellate court in the country.

*Sweatt, McLaurin,* and *Henderson* were scheduled for argument together, as if the Court viewed the three cases as presenting one singular or connecting central thesis for the Court's consideration. *Henderson* was called first, followed by *McLaurin,* then *Sweatt.* Thurgood and W.J. Durham from Dallas, Texas, argued the *Sweatt* case; Belford Lawson, a prominent lawyer from Washington and husband to Marjorie McKenzie, the *Pittsburgh Courier* columnist, and Jawn Sandifer, a friend and lawyer from New York closely allied with the NAACP, argued the *Henderson* case, which was not under our control. Nonetheless, we also believed that the three cases were

bound by a central theme: the validity of racial discrimination under the circumstances. The issue in *Henderson*
was violation of Section 3.1 of the Interstate Commerce
Act, which made it illegal "to subject any particular person to any undue prejudice." In the other cases we sought
a more far-reaching holding: that the separate but equal
doctrine of *Plessy v. Ferguson* was conceived in error in
that on its face and in its application it did not and could
not meet the equal protection requisites of the Fourteenth Amendment, that it was conceived initially in a
transportation case and, although assumed, it had never
been determined by the Court that it was applicable to
education. And for the first time, the Justice Department
weighed in on our side, filing an amicus curiae brief in the
*Sweatt* and *McLaurin* cases and arguing that the federal
government had erred in its position on railroad segregation; *Plessy* was wrong.

All three cases were decided in our favor. The Court
ordered Heman Sweatt admitted to the University of
Texas, holding that the separate facilities offered by the
state could not afford educational opportunity equal to
that of the University of Texas Law School. The Court
pointed to qualities "incapable of objective measurement
which make for greatness in a law school—reputation of
the faculty, experience of the administrators, position and
influence of the alumni, standing in the community, tradition and prestige"—that characterized the University
of Texas Law School and were hardly duplicated in the
school that the state hastily established for black students.
In the case of George McLaurin, the Court held that
McLaurin's isolation from his classmates denied the es-

sential right to interact with other students in ways essential to learning and ordered the state-imposed restrictions on McLaurin lifted. Finally, in the *Henderson* case, the Court ruled that dining car segregation was in violation of Section 3.1 of the Interstate Commerce Act.

While the Court refused to explicitly overrule the separate but equal doctrine, these three rulings in effect left *Plessy* moribund. We were confident that segregation imposed by law was in its death throes. We were euphoric with optimism, certain that our job of securing equal citizen rights for blacks would soon be completed. We had to find the means now, however, to nail the coffin on segregation's legal sanction and bury it finally and forever.

*Chapter 5*

# The Road to *Brown*

Our next tasks were to attack segregation in the primary and secondary school systems, to undertake a final drive to eliminate segregation in transportation, and to implement the gains achieved in *Sweatt* and *McLaurin*. My assignment was to devise a persuasive formula that would convince the Supreme Court that black children who were required to attend segregated primary and secondary schools were being denied the Fourteenth Amendment's guaranty of equal educational opportunity. I did not believe that either the primacy of the intangibles in *Sweatt* or the vital necessity of the opportunity for intellectual intercourse with fellow students in *McLaurin* provided the solution. We could not rely on the prestige of the white schools, the prominence or reputation of the alumni or faculty, since except for certain select schools one school was supposedly the equivalent of similar schools in the system. I felt we needed some other ingredient to prevail.

Reading anything and everything relevant in my search for what was needed, I came across a study by Otto Klineberg, professor of psychology at Columbia University. The study involved a group of black children in the Philadelphia public school system whose parents were part of the massive black migration to the urban North during and after World War II. Klineberg's study showed that the longer the black children, initially enrolled in the segregated schools in the South and now attending public schools in Philadelphia, stayed in the Philadelphia school system, the higher they scored on standardized IQ and achievement tests administered by Philadelphia school authorities.

This seemed to provide the key I was looking for. I met with Professor Klineberg and explained to him that we were preparing to institute litigation attacking the dual primary and secondary school systems of the South, and that while gross disparities in per pupil expenditures and basic facilities could probably provide a basis for success, if the states undertook as a result of the litigation to narrow the gap in financial expenditures and facilities, success could be only temporary. To avoid securing only temporary success, we wanted to show that enforced racial segregation itself was the constitutional infirmity. I told him that his study seemed to support that thesis and asked him to become a witness when the case was tried. He declined the invitation, but directed me to Professor Kenneth Clark, professor of psychology at the City University of New York, who with his wife, Mamie, had done a doll study that might be what I needed.

At the time I had no knowledge of the Clarks or their work. I subsequently learned that both had obtained their doctorate in psychology from Columbia University under Professor Henry Garrett, who later became the only witness of prestige and intellectual substance the segregationists were able to put on the witness stand during the trials of the five state school segregation cases. Together the Clarks had established the Northside Center for Child Development in Harlem, designed to provide psychological and psychiatric therapy and emotional sustenance for children and families in Harlem—the first and only such institution in Harlem. Although Kenneth played an important role at Northside, running the institution was largely Mamie's responsibility, while he devoted his time principally to City University.

Kenneth agreed to see me and thereafter agreed to help. The latter is an understatement, for his involvement was critical to our success. Kenneth testified in the South Carolina and Virginia cases, and in the South Carolina case he gave the doll test to the children. He helped me in Virginia in the cross-examination of the school board social science witnesses. He secured some of the most prominent social scientists at the time to sign a brief filed in the United States Supreme Court in the school segregation cases to the effect that racial segregation had a deleterious effect on the educational development of black children. He helped me find social scientists where the trials were being held, both in the initial cases and in those cases brought after the 1954 decision, as we expanded the attack to de facto school segregation in the North. We therefore had no need to overburden any of those who had already testified as expert witnesses or make them professional witnesses.

The Clarks' doll test showed that racial discrimination inflicted psychological harm on black children at a very early age. Up to the time of this study it had not been known either that discrimination's impact was inflicted or that its effect was perceived so early. Black preschool children may have been tested by third parties, but in our cases the earliest age group tested was in kindergarten. The children were shown a black doll and a white one. They were asked to point to the prettier doll, the one they liked best, the good doll, the bad doll, the doll most like them. In nearly all cases the prettier, best, and good doll, the one most like them, was the white doll; the bad doll was invariably the black one.

The first of the school segregation cases to be tried was *Briggs v. Elliott*, the South Carolina case. The NAACP was fortunate to have in James M. Hinton an aggressive, dynamic leader of our South Carolina State Conference of NAACP branches. To be certain that launching a frontal assault on segregation had the support of our southern membership, Thurgood called a conference in New York on June 26–27, 1950; it was attended by NAACP lawyers and branch and state conference presidents from twenty-two states and the District of Columbia. The issue of an all-out attack on segregation per se—that the focus was now to be on the constitutional argument that segregation itself denied blacks their right to equal educational opportunity guaranteed by the Fourteenth Amendment—was thoroughly discussed and explored. A few lawyers disapproved, but all the nonlawyers fully endorsed the proposal.

Hinton returned to South Carolina and obtained approval from the parents of the children attending the elementary and secondary schools in Clarendon County to institute litigation. We received the names of the proposed litigants with their signed authorization for us to represent them in the lawsuit. As was my practice when the case would undoubtedly pose high local risks, before putting the complaint in final form, I made a special trip to South Carolina to meet with all the parents who had signed authorizations.

We met in a church in Summerton. The church was packed. I carefully went over each paragraph of the complaint, explaining the meaning in language they would understand. I told them that the case was an all-out attack on segregation in the Clarendon County schools and that the suit was seeking to have their children attend school with white children. I told them they should expect the white people to be bitterly opposed to the suit and to throw everything possible at them to stop it. I told them that those parents named in the lawsuit as suing on behalf of their named children should expect to be threatened and subjected to violence, and that even the safety of their families and homes was at risk. Those with local employment should expect to be fired. They had to know what they were getting themselves into.

Handling the suit was no risk to me; it was to them. They had to live in the community and face all the hazards. I ended by telling them that now understanding what they faced, anyone who wanted to withdraw should do so. No embarrassment or shame should come with that decision. Surprisingly, at least to me, only two parents decided not to continue with the litigation. I ended my talk by saying I realized the hazards those who joined in the litigation would face, but we felt the time had come when we had to fight segregation head-on. At that moment, a gray-headed sage sitting in the corner of the church said, "We wondered how long it would take you lawyers to reach that conclusion," a remark greeted with laughter and applause. To say I came away from that meeting encouraged and energized is an understatement.

As usual in our important cases, when we sought to make new law we would discuss the proposed approach with members of our National Legal Committee. Fortunately, some of the best legal minds in the country were willing to give time and thought to help us improve and strengthen our legal attack on racial segregation in education. The committee was composed of black and white men, law professors and those engaged in the practice of law, all committed to ending segregation. There were no holds barred. Every idea or concept offered was subjected to close scrutiny and often to withering attack. If the proposition could not be successfully defended against attack by the committee, it was felt, it could not survive court testing.

Of all the professions, the savagery with which lawyers and law professors attack each other's ideas is unique, I believe. In most academic disciplines, dismissing one's ideas as nonsense is taken personally. With members of our legal committee, there wasn't anything personal involved. It was the idea or concept that was subjected to hard-nosed scrutiny. Thurgood wanted me to expand the boundaries of the law and protected me from office politics and intrigue so that I would feel free to do this. He could be counted on to support whatever concept I proposed as long as I stood up to any attack leveled against it by our legal group.

As I now reflect on those days, the absence of women from that inner circle of cooperating lawyers and law professors is evident to me, but it never crossed my mind then. Marian Wynn Perry was a member of the legal staff, and Constance Motley was a very active member beginning in the late 1940s; but of the staff only Thurgood and I actively engaged in the conceptual analysis with the committee members in deciding on a proposal. I had to participate because in most cases my proposed concepts were being discussed.

The proposed use of social scientists' testimony came under fierce attack from the outset. A number of the most influential members of the committee scorned social science data as without substance, since it was not hard science, proved by tests in the laboratory, but merely the reactions of a group of people. My argument was that we had to take a chance on social science findings, since we had found no alternative, and I firmly believed that relying on social science evidence would work. Since they had nothing better to offer, I won the initial skirmish and began preparing for the trial of the South Carolina case using social science testimony and Kenneth's doll test.

Thurgood decided to help try the case, and he

arranged for us to have a house to ourselves in Charleston, the site of the trial, three weeks before the scheduled trial date. Thurgood, Kenneth Clark, and I left from New York by train, with Spottswood Robinson joining us in Richmond. The trip was uneventful until we got off the train in Charleston. Our baggage had been taken off the train, and we were waiting for transportation to our temporary residence when Kenneth in distressful agitation started inspecting the baggage, shouting, "Where're my dolls, where're my dolls?" Spots, who had met Kenneth for the first time when he boarded the train in Richmond the night before, had not been told about Kenneth's use of dolls to show the early impact of racial discrimination on black children. He gave me a withering look of disgust. Thurgood and I had a good laugh. Kenneth located his dolls, and Spottswood, informed about Kenneth's role, was able to relax.

We proceeded to the house that would be our residence until the trial was concluded. Kenneth spent the trial-preparation period administering the doll test to a sizable number of children representative of the black children enrolled in the Clarendon County public schools. Thurgood spent time with Kenneth, familiarizing himself with the test procedures. We were putting on a number of experts in addition to Kenneth to testify that the dual school system did not provide equal educational opportunity for black children in that it marked them as inferior to white children, thus fatally frustrating their ability to learn. We also planned to have educational experts testify about the concrete disparities between the white and black schools in every accepted measure of educational quality, such as funding, curriculum, quality and experience of teachers, and equipment.

Spottswood and I were to share the questioning of our witnesses, with me examining Kenneth Clark. Thurgood was to cross-examine the state's key defense witnesses, and to get the experience, I was to be allowed to cross-examine the noncritical state witnesses. Spottswood and I made a trial outline stating what we hoped to achieve from each of our witnesses and spelling out the questions we planned to ask each of them. As the witnesses arrived, we put to them the questions that we would ask them on the witness stand. We also tried to prepare them for harsh cross-examination by putting questions to them in a hostile tone of voice as though we were opposing counsel.

Our experts were never put on the defensive or made to appear uncomfortable in this case nor any of the others I tried. I believe that was the result of their own formidable qualifications and because my basic instruction was for them to testify on the witness stand only about what their expertise qualified them to discuss, and within that context to testify only about what they felt confident in defending. Under no circumstances should they, in a desire to help, be led into making some pronouncement that was outside their field or that they could not defend as experts. I told them that such statements were of no greater value than the opinions of any layman or nonexpert in the courtroom, and would compromise the credibility of their expert testimony. When the academics were assured that we did not want them to stretch their findings beyond what they felt was supportable, any initial reluctance or concern about testifying disappeared.

A few defense witnesses, apparently not being so advised or in arrogance, did venture outside their field of expertise in trying to justify the dual school system—and they paid for it, leaving the witness stand battered, bruised, and humiliated. Expert witnesses should realize that opposing counsel attempts to absorb as much knowledge in the expert's field as possible, concentrating particularly on the expert's activities and writings. The object is to try to be on par with the expert during the cross-examination, with this miscellaneous knowledge being discarded when the trial is concluded. Of course, some experts have such formidable reputations and their composure is so impregnable that they can venture outside their field with impunity. With such witnesses the opposing counsel's best strategy is to finish his examination as quickly as possible and move on. Most experts are not so daunting, and those the counsel makes pay.

We filed our complaint and appeared before Judge J. Waities Waring in Charleston, South Carolina, in November 1950, but since we were attacking the constitutionality of the state's segregation statute, convening a three-judge court was required, and the state attorney general had to take over the case to defend the state law. This meant the losing party could bypass the court of appeals and seek immediate review by the Supreme Court. When the filing of the lawsuit was publicly announced as being a direct attack on the constitutional validity of the traditional pattern of segregation in the South, South Carolina's governor James Byrnes, a former Supreme Court Justice, bluntly stated: "South Carolina will abolish the public school system before allowing Negroes and whites to attend the same schools." As the litigation progressed, the governor announced the launching of a $75 million program to equalize the black schools.

The case was tried in Judge Waring's courtroom in Charleston. In addition to Judge Waring, the judges were John J. Parker, chief judge of the Court of Appeals for the Fourth Circuit, and United States district judge George Bell Timmerman. In 1930, Judge Parker had been nominated by President Herbert Hoover to sit on the Supreme Court. His nomination was fiercely opposed by the NAACP and other organizations for an earlier remark questioning the fitness of blacks to exercise the right to vote. The Senate refused to confirm his nomination. Since that time Judge Parker had consistently upheld the citizenship rights of blacks in a wide range of cases brought before him, including education, suffrage, equalization of teachers' salaries, discrimination involving railroad passengers, and employment. Judge Waring was a bona fide progressive, in contrast to Judge Timmerman, who was a typical southern judge.

As with all our court trials during that period, this one was public theater. The courtroom was filled to overflowing with black spectators. The trial was of intense interest because of its attack on school segregation and because spectators would have the opportunity to see the legendary Thurgood Marshall in action. He did not disappoint. His primary defense witness to cross-examine was the superintendent of schools, who had the misfortune of having Crow as his surname. Thurgood was born and reared in Maryland and normally spoke with a mild southern drawl. When in a courtroom in the South that drawl became very pronounced, with a timbre not of the upper South but of rural Georgia or Alabama.

He put the superintendent under withering cross-examination, and as he forced the witness to admit to each disparity under discussion, he would end the sentence pronouncing Mr. Crow's name, allowing the blacks in the audience to supply the nuance "Jim" to Mr. Crow. The black spectators were delighted with his performance. The trial was unique in that it was the only time Kenneth gave his doll test to the plaintiffs in the lawsuit, so that his testimony was specific as to impairment in the ability of the plaintiffs to learn, which his tests showed resulted from racial segregation in the Clarendon County school system. It was the only one of the cases Thurgood participated in at the trial level.

The state did not put up much of a defense. Governor Byrnes had decided to undertake a massive program of building and funding to lower the gap between the black and white schools to come within the parameters of *Plessy v. Ferguson*'s separate but equal mandate. In the beginning I believe southern officials thought the dual school system would readily survive our legal attack. Racial segregation was touted in the press and by public officials as the South's way of life, a critical element of southern life in place for one hundred years, and that it would survive for one hundred or two hundred more.

That segregation had been in place for one hundred years or more was a myth. In most southern states racial segregation had been imposed by law only after the 1876 Tilden-Hayes compromise pursuant to which Hayes was allowed to become president and federal troops were withdrawn from the South, with southern Bourbons being given license to deal with freed blacks without interference from the North. This led to a period of black disenfranchisement, suppression, wholesale violence, burning of entire towns where blacks were evidencing signs of economic well-being, lynchings, and the reimposition of the vestiges of slavery. In this environment, racial segregation was imposed by law, which meant the segregation statutes were only fifty or sixty years old.

On June 21, 1951, the trial court rendered a 2–1 decision refusing to enjoin continuation of the dual school system, holding that the system was not in and of itself in violation of the Fourteenth Amendment, but found that the facilities for black children were not equal to those provided for white children. The court ordered the defendants to proceed at once to provide equal facilities for black children and to report back to the court within six months as to what action had been taken by them to carry out the court's order. In his dissent, Judge Waring held that we had shown the unconstitutionality of the dual school system and were entitled to an injunction dismantling the system.

During my tenure no lawyer on the legal staff ever had the luxury of having only one case on his or her calendar. Each of us was always handling a number of legal matters simultaneously. In addition to the school desegregation case, I also had on my plate the court-martial appeal of the convictions of Herman Dennis, Calvin Dennis, and Robert Burns in the Guam rape case from 1949 and 1950. This case, in which the lives of two men hung in the balance, was a deeply emotional undertaking for me and—

amid the trials and final preparation of the argument in the Supreme Court of the school segregation cases—consumed much of my energies.

In the intervening years, we had exhausted the military appeal process, and in early January 1952 we were notified that the air force judge advocate general had approved the decisions of the ultimate and final appellate body in the air force judicial hierarchy denying our petitions for new trial or other relief. I was advised that official notification of the decision would be withheld from the men for two weeks, during which time we were asked to advise the judge advocate general whether we planned to take other action in the cases. We advised the judge advocate general that we planned to proceed in the federal courts seeking writs of habeas corpus on behalf of the three accused, and on January 31, 1952, we filed the requisite petition in the United States District Court for the District of Columbia on behalf of Burns and Herman Dennis. In the interim the Judicial Council had commuted the death sentence of Calvin Dennis to life.

We filed a petition for writ of habeas corpus in U.S. District Court for the District of Columbia. The petition sought the men's release from military custody on the grounds that the trials and convictions of the two men violated their rights to a fair trial because they were convicted by the use of perjured testimony, coerced confessions, and the use of other illegal evidence; because of prosecutorial misconduct alleged in the trial judge advocate's intimidating of the accused and of witnesses who sought to give testimony favorable to the defense, and planting evidence to show the guilt of the accused and suppressing evidence favorable to the men; and because the accused were denied the right to effective assistance of counsel and were tried in an atmosphere of hostility, hysteria, and violence that made a fair and impartial hearing impossible. We were aided by the judge advocate general in securing affidavits needed to support the petition.

I should note here that the Washington military personnel administering the appeals process treated me with the utmost courtesy and consideration. Every request made was granted; every document asked for was provided. The identity of all relevant military personnel involved in the investigation, in bringing the charges, or in the court-martial was readily supplied. When additional time was needed, it was given. The courteous consideration and cooperation during the year or so I processed the military appeal have not been exceeded by any court or agency personnel before whom I practiced in the entire twenty-seven years of my legal career.

A hearing and argument was held in the district court in March 1952, and in April it denied the petition. We appealed to the Court of Appeals for the District of Columbia Circuit, which granted a stay of execution pending decision on the appeal. A three-judge panel heard arguments in June 1952, and on July 31, 1952, in a 2–1 decision, with Judge Bazelon dissenting, affirmed the decision of the district court. The majority concluded that the facts alleged did not supply grounds for granting the relief sought. The court found the lack-of-counsel claim unwarranted, pointing to our representation in the military appellate process "by the same counsel who so ably presented this appeal" as foreclosing any claim of lack of adequate counsel. This was the first time my skill had been used against my client.

A further stay of execution was granted for sixty days for us to file a petition for writ of certiorari seeking review by the Supreme Court. Review was granted and the case was argued before the high court on February 4, 1953. Frank Reeves helped prepare the Supreme Court brief and was at the counsel table during the argument to be sure all our points were adequately covered. This was my third argument before the Court. My head and heart were so exclusively engaged in trying to persuade the justices that these men had suffered a grave miscarriage of justice that the Court could and should right that there was no space for nervousness. Unfortunately, the effort was to no avail, and the Court in the week of June 21, 1953, held in a 6–3 decision that we were not entitled to a civil court hearing to challenge the validity of the court-martial convictions. We filed a petition for rehearing, which we knew would merely delay the finality of the decision until October 1953.

The case had stirred considerable attention in the black community and press. Blacks being killed—lynched by white mobs or sentenced to death by all-white juries in summary court trials lacking any semblance of due process—was commonplace. The black community had become conditioned to view claims of black rape of a white as false. The black community and press fully supported our attempt to get the court-martial convictions set aside. After our court effort failed, Mrs. Robert L. Vann, the president and publisher of the *Pittsburgh Courier*, convinced by the paper's own investigation that the men had not received a fair trial, tried to use her influence to secure presidential intervention, but without success. Pertinent parts of her letter to the president were published in the newspaper. In addition, she urged her readers to join her in writing the president, asking him to order an independent fact-finding review before final implementation of the convictions and sentences. The editor of the paper, William Nunn, refused to believe the president ever saw the letter; he was convinced that it had been intercepted by a member of the White House staff and never reached the president.

I am not wedded to that belief. It must be remembered that President Eisenhower was a part of the same military culture as the officers who decided the men's fate in the initial court-martial trials. As commanding general of the army, he had vehemently opposed President Truman's order to integrate the armed services and believed that the South's pattern of segregation was appropriate. Finally, it was with great reluctance that he ordered federal troops to Little Rock, Arkansas, to enforce the Supreme Court's decree requiring the admission of black children to the heretofore white public school. Southern culture on the issue of race relations was too embedded in him to give me reason to believe that if the letter had reached him, he would have acted.

William Nunn did receive a letter from Max Raab, a member of the White House staff, reacting to the sharp criticisms of the military and the White House's failure to intervene. Raab sought suggestions from Nunn on how to avoid in the future miscarriages of justice similar to those in this case. In a letter to me dated February 19,

1954, Nunn solicited my help. I suggested that the accused be afforded the right to prove his case, to confront witnesses who contested his version of the facts, to have access to the report of the military investigation and to all the evidence and testimony before the military on which its decision is based.

I must have received notice that all had been lost in the midst of preparing for the *Brown* case. This is the only case I lost in argument before the Supreme Court. I wish, of course, the failure had not come at the expense of two men's lives.

Robert Burns was the strongest in character of the three and seemed least likely to be involved in the crime for which he was tried and convicted. He had an alibi placing him nowhere near the scene and swore that the first contact he had with either Herman or Calvin was on meeting them in the Guam jail. He was the most respected and admired by the people who solicited our intervention. Unlike the other two men, despite the beatings, threats, and false promises, he never confessed to involvement in the crime. Herman broke under the beatings and torture they were put through by the Guam security officials, but he recanted before his court-martial trial and never testified that he, Burns, or Calvin victimized Ruth Farnsworth. We kept their and our own hopes alive for four years that we would succeed in securing a just result, and their letters to me, especially those from Burns, were fulsome with gratitude for what we were doing and for the persistence of our efforts. In consistently assuring us of ultimate success, Burns probably kept our hopes alive, as much as our persistence contributed to his and Herman's own hopes.

The youngest of the three, Calvin succumbed and at his court-martial implicated Herman and Burns and denied that he had been physically abused. After learning that he had been lied to and that promises of leniency were false—since his own court-martial resulted in his conviction and imposition of the death penalty, the same as Burns's and Herman's—he recanted, relating the gruesome story of physical and psychological abuse, plus false promises for his perjured testimony. By then it was too late for them or us. Without his testimony we might have had a chance, if not in the military, then in the federal courts.

I was writing the *Brown* brief when news of Burns's execution was relayed to me. I did not have time to grieve until later, which was personally unfortunate. If I can express emotion of whatever kind, it helps. Then I am free of it. When I am unable to do so, as in this instance, it seems to stay with me forever. So every time my thoughts turn to Burns's execution, I grieve. In what way did I fail to do what might have saved his life? This was the only case in my career that I was not able as a professional to work on at a remove. I became so emotionally involved, so fervently convinced of the innocence of my clients and so personally committed to saving their lives, that the notification of failure almost broke my heart. Recovery took time, and fortunately, I was kept busy over the next several years. But even now, after the passage of fifty years, emotion wells up as I attempt to revisit and record the events, and I again ask myself as I did fifty years ago, "Could I have done a better job?"

We became involved in the school segregation case in Topeka, Kansas, late in the summer of 1950, when the local branch decided to litigate. In Kansas at the time urban school districts of a certain size were permitted to maintain segregated schools. The statute gave final authority to the local school district to make the decision on whether to segregate or not. The Topeka school board had decided to maintain a dual elementary school system. The black parents complained about the quality of the physical facilities and educational offerings in the schools their children were required to attend.

Unlike the South Carolina case, which had been financed by the state NAACP, we found that no effort had been made to raise the necessary funds to underwrite costs of the Topeka litigation. Nonetheless, we decided to proceed. We were already litigating a case from the Deep South and we were certain of one from Virginia. Our people in Louisiana, Georgia, Florida, and Alabama thought they might have a case ready shortly. Kansas, a border state that permitted various school boards to segregate, was an ideal addition to our effort to reveal the compulsory nature of the dual school system in the Deep South. We might get a ruling in our favor, or a different kind of analysis of the problem than we could expect from the Deep South, since the permissive nature of the segregated school system in Topeka meant there was less pressure to maintain it than in states like South Carolina, Georgia, and Virginia.

I sent what I thought was a final draft of the complaint in mid-December 1950, but differences with local counsel over language delayed the filing until March 1951, and I had to amend the complaint in May 1951. I decided to take Jack Greenberg with me to try the case, his first. He was given the task of doing all the basic pretrial preparation. We secured the services of Dr. Hugh W. Speer, chairman of the Department of Education at the University of Kansas City, to do a survey of the elementary white and black schools in Topeka, Kansas. There were seven all-white and four all-black schools in Topeka at the time.

We wanted to keep our expenses as limited as possible. We sought to secure the needed expert witnesses from Kansas City's academic community at the University of Kansas in Lawrence, which is roughly sixty-five miles from Topeka. Acting on Dr. Speer's suggestions and with his assistance, Jack succeeded in lining up ten expert witnesses. These people did not increase our expenses very much, since they testified for us in the case as a public service and sought only reimbursement for their expenses.*

Topeka maintained segregated public accommodations, so I had to stay in a hotel for blacks. It was a horri-

---

* In addition to these local people the ten included Dr. Horace English, who operated a psychological clinic at Ohio State University in Columbus, Ohio; Associate Professor Max L. Huff of the Department of Psychology at the University of Michigan; Professor John J. Kane of the Department of Sociology at the University of Notre Dame; and Professor W.B. Brookover of the Department of Social Science at Michigan State University.

ble place. I urged Jack to stay in the main hotel, but he refused. Our room was dirty, with wallpaper torn off and hanging from the walls. The bathtub looked as if it had never been cleaned, and we had to scrub it with soap, Ajax, and Lysol to use it. We had to make the best of it. Jack and I were on friendly terms; I had taken him under my wing and was at his side as he handled his first trial. He earned credits from me for not following my advice. On reflection he really had no choice but to stay. While I would not have faulted him for not staying in that miserable hotel room with me, the NAACP personnel would have thought ill of him, and Jack probably realized that. Plus he probably did not believe that I would not hold it against him if he followed my suggestion and moved out. But I did not believe then or now that anyone who could go elsewhere in place of that miserable, unsavory room should be faulted for doing so.

The trial began on June 25, 1951, before a three-judge court, chaired by Judge Walter Huxman of the Tenth Circuit Court of Appeals, accompanied by Judges Arthur Mellott and Delmas Hill of the U.S. District Court. Jack handled the direct case, while I did most of the examination of our experts and the cross-examination, and made the closing argument.

The trial was relatively uneventful. As usual, black spectators filled the courtroom. We made a good record. Dr. Speer and his assistants had done a detailed survey of the two sets of schools, and their testimony showed that in every measurable relevant educational criterion, the schools assigned to black children were far inferior to the schools set aside for white children. Our experts empha-

William Hastie, one of my early role models. Among
the many positions he held during a long career, Hastie
served as dean of Howard Law School, the first black governor of the Virgin Islands, and the first black appointed
to the federal court of appeals, a position he held for
twenty-one years.

Charles McLaurin, plaintiff in *McLaurin v. Oklahoma State Regent*, seated in a classroom at the University of Oklahoma. The makeshift arrangements for segregating McLaurin helped us to broaden our challenge to the fiction of "separate but equal."

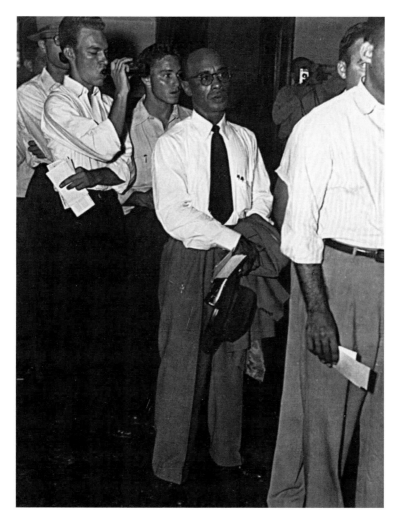

Heman Sweatt, plaintiff in *Sweatt v. Painter*, who was ordered admitted to the University of Texas in 1950.

The author in November 1951 with Mack Ingram, a sharecropper tried for assaulting Miss Willie Jean Boswell with the intent to rape. At the trial, it was established that the forty-four-year-old Ingram came no closer than seventy-five feet from the young girl. A mistrial was declared on November 16, when the jury was deadlocked ten to two for conviction, with two of the four black members holding out for acquittal.

The attorneys in *Brown v. Board of Education*. I am standing second from left. Courtesy of the NAACP Legal Defense and Educational Fund, Inc.

A photograph taken in the late 1950s, during my tenure as NAACP General Counsel.

The author addresses a dinner in Charleston, South Carolina, in 1955 honoring J. Waties Waring, the federal judge who ruled in favor of overturning school segregation in *Briggs v. Elliot* and also struck down the white primary in South Carolina. Courtesy of the South Caroliniana Library, University of South Carolina, Columbia; from the Arthur J. Clement Papers.

My wife, Gloria Carter, on the beach in Jamaica in the late 1960s.

My two sons, John and David, standing behind me and my mother, Annie Martin Carter. This is the only extant photograph of her.

On vacation in Jamaica with Derrick Bell and Kenneth Clark.

sized the damage segregation did to the ability of the black children to learn.

Some of the most effective testimony was given by Louisa Holt, who was a professor of social psychology at the University of Kansas. She lived in Topeka and her two children attended the public schools. She spoke of the psychological damage segregation inflicted not only on black children but on her children and other white children as well, since the latter were not exposed to other groups and would be handicapped later in life when their careers required working in diverse ethnic settings.

Jack and Charles Scott, local NAACP counsel, did an excellent job of getting the parents through their testimony in good shape and in putting on the major elements of our direct case. They were then in a law firm with their father, Elisha, who was a legendary figure in local legal circles. He had been an outstanding criminal lawyer, winning such cases as the Tulsa, Oklahoma, riot case, the Coffeeville riot cases, and the Leavenworth Disciplinary Barracks riot cases. All of these had followed the usual pattern: clashes between whites and blacks erupted in violence resulting in injury or death and destruction of property, and in the aftermath only the black participants faced criminal prosecution. Elisha Scott gained a reputation of having never lost a criminal case. Unfortunately, he had now become an alcoholic.

We made final preparations for the trial in the Scotts' office. Elisha was never present and had said not a word to me about the case. He did, however, make a bizarre appearance during the cross-examination of Dr. Speer, who on direct examination had testified concerning the inequalities in facilities between the white and black elementary schools in Topeka. Speer stated that adjoining the school's campus was a demonstration school in which black children attended school with white children, and the children seemed very happy. Elisha walked in and objected to this statement, saying, "He is evading the rights and he is answering a question not based on the evidence adduced or that could be adduced." Judge Huxman asked if he was counsel of record. Elisha said he was supposed to be. The judge allowed him to make the objection and then overruled it. Elisha was visibly close to being drunk. I was horrified, embarrassed, and angry, wondering how badly we had been hurt, how I could silence him, and whether the court would blame us. It was over very quickly, but it seemed to go on for a long time. Elisha left the courtroom after the judge overruled his objection, and I never saw him again. The trial resumed as if there had been no bizarre interruption.

The trial concluded in three days and Judge Huxman put us on a fast track. We had to file our brief by July 20, 1951, giving me hope that the decision by the court would come in early August. On June 29, 1951, I wrote a memo to Thurgood telling him that we should try to get the Topeka and South Carolina cases to the Supreme Court at the same time. Given the number of strong witnesses testifying in support of our position, the record in Topeka was better than the one in South Carolina; the two cases would be excellent supplements for each other.

The Kansas decision did come down in August, and it was a moral victory for us. The court ruled against us, since it felt *Plessy v. Ferguson* had not been overruled. It did find that segregation was harmful, and it had difficulty distinguishing this case from *McLaurin* and *Sweatt* on segregation being a denial of equal protection of the laws, but said that perhaps the doctrine in those cases was limited to graduate and professional schools.

We had appealed the trial court's decision immediately in the South Carolina case, and it was docketed for consideration by the Supreme Court in its October 1951 term. When the decision in Topeka came down in mid-August, we put the appeal on a very fast track and were able to get the appeal papers filed in the Supreme Court for consideration in its October 1951 term along with the South Carolina appeal.

While the South Carolina appeal was pending, defendants filed in the district court the report that the trial court had ordered submitted. The report stated provisions had been made for massive schoolhouse construction. The state legislature had passed legislation to enable the local school board to secure the funds needed to equalize the school facilities by incurring bonded indebtedness of up to 30 percent of the assessed value of all taxable property within the district. The report asserted that teachers' salaries had been equalized, as had the curricula, and that $21,522.81 had already been spent for tables, chairs, and desks and for improving existing black school buildings pending the construction and occupancy of those that were being and would be constructed. The defendants asked for time to complete the program, which they assured the court would provide equal facilities for black schoolchildren.

Since the appeal had brought the case to the jurisdic-

tion of the Supreme Court, the lower court did not consider the report. On January 28, 1952, the Supreme
Court took up the South Carolina appeal. In a per curiam
opinion, the Supreme Court vacated the lower court decision and sent the case back to the lower court to take
whatever action it deemed appropriate. Justices Hugo
Black and William Douglas dissented, holding that, as
"additional facts contained in the report to the District
Court are wholly irrelevant to the constitutional questions presented by the appeal to this Court, we should
note jurisdiction and set the case down for argument." On
January 31, 1952, we filed a motion for mandamus, and
on February 4 the Court issued a mandate ordering the
lower court to proceed immediately with a second hearing. On February 7 we moved for final judgment on the
grounds that the children could get no immediate relief
except by issuance of an injunction enjoining enforcement of racial segregation. Following a second hearing,
the lower court issued its judgment on March 3, again up-
holding segregation by the same 2–1 vote. On May 10 we
filed a statement of jurisdiction, again asking for review
by the Supreme Court.

In the Topeka case the statement of jurisdiction was
initially filed in October 1951 and was on the Court's
docket at the same time the South Carolina case was sent
back to the lower court. The assistant attorney general of
Kansas, Paul Wilson, was a reluctant participant and had
to be ordered by the Court to present his views, on which
basis the Court may have held up consideration. Apparently he did present his views, and the case moved ahead

of South Carolina in the 1952 Court term. Our brief on the merits was filed on September 23, 1952.

The Virginia case (*Davis v. Prince Edward County*) was probably our best effort involving enforced racial segregation in the high schools in the country. The judges were Armistead M. Dobie of the Fourth Circuit and Sterling Hutcheson and Albert V. Bryan of the U.S. District Court. It was considered the most comprehensive education suit we had presented thus far. We had experts in psychology, psychiatry, sociology, anthropology, education, and statistics testify in our direct case, plus four rebuttal witnesses to challenge testimony of state witnesses, including a statistician who testified that the equalization proposed by the state could not possibly be completed until 1979.

I had fun destroying the credibility and composure of a state witness whose field was psychiatry. He offered a number of critical opinions about the lack of harm to the children from segregation. On cross-examination I determined that he had no qualifications as a psychologist. When he was giving opinions about the lack of harm caused by segregation, he was speaking outside his field. He sputtered in response to my queries, and in an attempt to show contempt and disdain, I took my seat. I am not certain how well my little dramatic act registered, since drama is not my style, but he looked upset.

We had not abandoned the denial-of-equal-facilities argument. As of 1951 the average per pupil expenditure in nine southern states—Alabama, Arkansas, Florida, Georgia, Maryland, Mississippi, North Carolina, Oklahoma, and South Carolina—was $135.60 for whites, $74.50 for blacks; the per pupil value of school property was $301.29 for whites, $81.93 for blacks; transportation expenditure per pupil was $10.40 for whites, $2.45 for blacks. For South Carolina alone the per pupil expenditures were $146.42 for whites, $67.05 for blacks; the per pupil value of school property were $285.40 for whites, $66.05 for blacks; and per pupil transportation expenditures were $9.67 for whites, $1.03 for blacks. Dr. Charles H. Thompson, dean of the Graduate School at Howard University and our principal expert in education, said that at the current rate of progress in attempting to close the gap, it would take eighty-four more years to equalize the median years of schooling for the two groups.

Initially the Court had scheduled oral arguments for *Brown* and *Briggs* for October 8, 1952. The arguments were postponed to December. The Court ordered the *Davis* case placed on its docket, bypassing the United States Court of Appeals, and consolidated it with all the school segregation cases to be heard, including one from the District of Columbia and the two cases from Delaware, which Jack Greenberg and Louis Redding had tried. We worked intensely from late summer through the fall preparing and revising the briefs. There was still considerable disagreement regarding how heavily we should rely upon social science evidence. Kenneth Clark's use of dolls and his social science findings were ridiculed by several of the lawyers; Bill Coleman was particularly harsh. I defended Kenneth and challenged Bill and the rest to give us an alternative, which they were unable to supply. I told the group that I thought the social scientists and Dr. Clark provided what we needed, and that we were going to rely on that approach.

Thirty-two psychiatrists, psychologists, educators, sociologists, and anthropologists signed a statement as an appendix to our brief; all of the signers agreed that "regardless of the facilities which are provided, enforced segregation is psychologically detrimental to the segregated group" and to the white majority as well, and that segregation has been and could be eliminated without "outbreaks of violence."*

On Tuesday, December 9, 1952, I began our presentation before the Court. My assignment was to argue and

---

* Those signing were Professor Floyd H. Allport, University of Syracuse; Professor Gordon W. Allport, Harvard University; Charlotte Babcock, M.D., Chicago; Viola W. Bernard, M.D., New York; Professor James S. Bruner, Harvard University; Professor Hadley Cantril, Princeton University; Professor Isidor Chein, NYU; Professor Kenneth Clark, College of the City of New York; Dr. Mamie P. Clark, Northside Center for Child Development, New York; Professor Stuart W. Cook, NYU; Professor Bingham Dai, Duke University Medical School; Professor Allison Davis, University of Chicago; Professor Else Frenkel-Brunswik, University of California; Professor Noel P. Gist, University of Missouri; Professor Daniel Katz, University of Michigan; Professor Otto Klineberg, Columbia University; Professor David Krech, University of California; Professor Alfred McClung Lee, Brooklyn College; Professor R.M. MacIver, Columbia University; Professor Robert K. Marton, NYU; Professor Gardner Murphy, Menninger Clinic, Topeka, Kansas; Professor Theodore M. Newcomb, University of Michigan; Professor Robert Redfield, University of Chicago; Professor Ira DeA. Reid, Haverford College; Professor Arnold M. Rose, University of Minnesota; Professor Gerhart Saenger, NYU; Professor R. Newitt, Vassar College; Professor S. Stanfield Sargent, Barnard College; Professor M. Brewster Smith, Social Science Research Council, New York; Professor Samuel A. Stouffer, Harvard University; Professor Wellman Warner, NYU; and Professor Robin M. Williams, Cornell University.

defend our position on the constitutional issue. While I was no longer the novice of two years ago, mine was a critical task and a heavy responsibility, since the outcome of all of the five cases and the case from the District of Columbia hinged on whether I could persuade the Court to accept my contention and overrule *Plessy v. Ferguson*, dealing the separate but equal doctrine a final deathblow.

The heart of my argument was that the separate but equal doctrine had been first applied to a transportation case and thereafter applied to a number of school cases without independent analysis to determine whether it could properly govern equal opportunity in school facility cases. Frankfurter challenged my analysis, pointing out that over the years very able and distinguished jurists had applied the doctrine to educational cases, even listing the names of some of the justices who had done so. I agreed, but countered that these justices had done no independent analysis of their own. They had assumed a prior Court had done so, but no prior Court had. This Court now had the opportunity, and when it made its independent analysis, it would agree with me that the doctrine could not provide equal educational opportunity for black children as the Constitution requires.

When Frankfurter could not make me back off my position, he relaxed and I believe he said, "You mean there is no rational basis for classification based on race." Whether he made that concession or by gesture indicated that he was satisfied, he indicated that I had done what he wanted done. Frankfurter did not ask idle questions. They were put to make a point—sometimes, as he would say to me from time to time, to explore the implications of the issues and to reveal the full effect of what would result if we prevailed. In this case, since the Court accepted and incorporated my argument in Chief Justice Warren's opinion, Frankfurter's questioning could have been to see whether my argument could be defended or whether he could make me bend.

After completing the constitutional phase of the argument, I spent the rest of my hour giving a factual picture of the Topeka school system. Paul Wilson, the assistant attorney general for the state of Kansas, was not really fully committed to defending segregation in Topeka. He made no impassioned defense of the system. He merely argued that the statute was within the state's power to enact and nothing in the federal constitution prevented it.

Next came the plaintiff's argument in the South Carolina and Virginia cases, which were argued together, with Thurgood and Spottswood making their presentations. I thought Thurgood was in particularly good form. He did not spend much time on the facts, which did not seem to engender much interest in the Court. He emphasized that the unfulfilled promise of American democracy to African Americans had to be met, that equal opportunity for blacks needed to be satisfied. He was in effect wrapping the American flag around himself and waving it throughout his argument. It was a very moving performance, especially for the black people in the audience. Spots was Spots—he gave a straight account of the facts, the details of which he had at his fingertips.

J. Lindsay Almond, the attorney general for Virginia, took over the defense of Virginia. His was the expected segregationist fire and brimstone, with moderation. John

Davis argued the case for South Carolina. At the time Davis was touted as the country's most eminent lawyer. He was reputed to have an unmatched record of successes in the high court. We were told by some of Davis's admirers that he was a liberal and had agreed to take the case with great reluctance and because of his friendship with Governor Byrnes. We all waited with more than ordinary interest to hear the argument. There was no apprehension, at least not on my part. If he was able to persuade the Court to rule against us, we would merely be frozen in the status quo and would have to try again. We would lose if we could not persuade the Court to reject the separate but equal doctrine, which was where we stood now.

When Davis began his presentation, I lost all respect for him. His was a mean-spirited approach, intended to demean and humiliate. Blacks should be happy to live under South Carolina's enforced segregated environment. They were being misled by unscrupulous advisers and now in greed they risked losing the benefits the state had showered on them. They were like the dog with the bone, who looks in the river and sees his reflection, but thinking it another dog with a bigger bone lets go of his and loses all. As I recall, the justices heard him in silence.

Since that experience, I have been before the Court many times and had to listen to many offensive arguments in defense of racial segregation and discrimination, but I have heard no argument that engendered the anger and disgust I felt hearing Davis. Too many white people in this country share Davis's sentiment that blacks should be content with half a loaf or even a quarter of a loaf of full equality. In time your dreams will come true. When you inquire whether they would follow that advice if in our position, they are truly puzzled that you put that question, because they cannot visualize being in a black person's position, as their whiteness makes that impossible to consider.

As I recall, the two Delaware cases were not allotted full time, but Jack Greenberg and Louis Redding were heard briefly. The District of Columbia school case presentation closed the hearing on the merits in the school segregation cases.

The order came down in June 1953 to reargue the cases. We were asked to answer five questions about the intent of the framers of the Fourteenth Amendment regarding segregated schools. We engaged John A. Davis to oversee the nonlegal research. He secured a formidable group of political scientists, historians, educators, and social scientists to help. Thurgood worked with John, doing that part of the brief that answered the questions the Court had asked. My job was to prepare the constitutional argument and to work with Kenneth Clark's group of social scientists. Before the deadline for filing our brief was reached, in September 1953 Chief Justice Fred Vinson died; Earl Warren, former governor of California, was named to succeed him and was confirmed in October 1953. The reargument was then scheduled for December 1953.

We had worked during the summer on the issues involved and had engaged educators, historians, and political and social scientists to undertake research on specific issues and to provide us with monographs setting forth their conclusions. We asked these scholars—whose work had touched upon the Civil War and its aftermath, or who had engaged in any research or study relevant to the issues we faced in these cases—to come to New York from September 14–18, 1953, to meet with fellow colleagues and lawyers to aid in the preparation of our brief. The response was extremely gratifying; a formidable group of the most brilliant scholars in their respective fields gathered in New York on September 14, and most did not leave until the end. They included John Hope Franklin, Rayford Logan, C. Vann Woodward, and Alfred Kelly.

The conference began with a plenary session in the Warwick Hotel, a midtown hotel about a block away from our offices on West Forty-third Street. At the meeting the scholars who had undertaken specific assignments for us presented their papers to the group. Suggestions and possible alternative approaches were proposed. We adhered to a time limit for discussion of each paper. The lawyers, particularly those scheduled to argue, were getting a valuable preparatory education. Beginning the next day and for several days thereafter we met in smaller groups for intense discussion centered on each of the presentations at the plenary session.

My presentation concerned the constitutional cases where the Court had overruled prior decisions, showing the fluidity of constitutional interpretation resulting from new understanding and changed conditions. My study covered every relevant case. In addition, I reviewed the history of the separate but equal doctrine, first applied in a transportation case and thereafter applied to education cases without the Court examining whether the doctrine could be applied to education and provide equal educational opportunity to blacks, which the Fourteenth Amendment required. I wanted to argue that with the opportunity now presenting itself to the Court for the first time, we were certain that on examination it would be found that the doctrine had no applicability to education and the doctrine should be overruled. There was considerable interest in these issues among the educators, historians, political scientists, and social scientists present. We spent about two days of intense discussion on this issue and the history of the black experience, all of which informed my brief and argument before the Court.

On the afternoon of September 18 we closed the conference with a plenary session, this time at the Association of the Bar of the City of New York, about a block from our offices. The presenters summarized what their final conclusions were or were hoped to be after completion of the additional inquiries the panel agreed should be undertaken. This had been for me, and I believe for most of the staff, one of the most exhilarating intellectual experiences we had ever had. As a result, our brief was an outstanding document, and our presentation to the Court was sure to be well informed—and, in Thurgood's case, brilliant.

We submitted on behalf of the plaintiffs only one brief on the merits for all five of the state cases, supplemented with the social science appendix setting forth the view of the adverse effects of enforced segregation and on an assurance that its elimination would not result in violence. An appendix set forth in detail the raw data of our research. The first part of the brief, written by me, contained the constitutional argument, including the analysis of the separate but equal doctrine that in our view governed the determination of the five cases and the discussion of the facts in the Topeka case (*Brown v. Board of Education*), the South Carolina case (*Briggs v. Elliott*), the Virginia case (*Davis v. Prince Edward County School Board*), and one of the Delaware cases decided in our favor (*Gebhart v. Belton*). The second Delaware case also decided in our favor came down before the Supreme Court argument and was joined with the others for decision. The rest of the brief, written by Thurgood and Spottswood, discussed and summarized our findings and conclusions regarding the questions the Court had asked the parties. The final part of the brief discussed the remedy we sought.

The brief for the District of Columbia case was submitted as a separate document written by George E.C. Hayes—who possessed one of the most skillful and elegant trial techniques I have ever seen—and James Nabrit, who later became president of Howard University. We argued that while the Fifth Amendment (which was applicable, since the federal and not the state government was involved) contained no equal protection clause, Court precedent made clear that the equal protection clause of the Fourteenth Amendment had been incorporated therein and made an integral part of the Fifth Amendment.

By the time the case was reargued on December 7–8, 1953, the Topeka School Board had volunteered to desegregate its schools. My presentation before the Court began with Justice Frankfurter asking after only a few sentences into my argument whether my case was moot. My reply was that I hoped I would get a little further in the argument before that question was asked. The court-room burst into laughter and Justice Frankfurter laughed and seemed to enjoy it. Justice Jackson came to my rescue with a question that allowed me to point out that while the state said it would admit the children to a desegre-gated school all but one was still attending segregated schools.

The case appeared to be moot since the state of Kansas did not defend the policy of segregation but had not ef-fected full desegregation. I expressed doubts, but I would not press the matter further.

At the end of the Supreme Court session in 1953, all of us were mentally and physically fatigued. I was too tired to have any sensible thought in mind other than re-laxing with family and friends with some good food and drinks, swapping stories based on nonsense. I was guard-edly optimistic—or perhaps hopeful more accurately de-scribes the mood. I thought we had a majority of the Court with us and Warren was a plus since we could not have counted on Chief Justice Vinson being on our side. The fact that the Court had brought all the school segre-gations cases up for dispositon was a good sign that the Court was prepared to make a major race relations' dis-positive ruling, and I could not believe it would uphold segregation.

Ours had been a summer and fall of concentrated work. We had worked twelve- to sixteen-hour days. Our secretarial help had had to work overtime most of that pe-riod. It was late December before I could take my own va-cation, since I had to let all the other lawyers take time off first. I had to monitor the office for two weeks or so, but there was not much to do. One of the things I remember doing during that December 1953 vacation was going to Detroit to see the Cleveland Browns play the Detroit Lions in the National Football League championship. I was a Browns fan, and went to the game confident my team would win, only to be devastated by Bobby Layne's passing skills. That was a huge disappointment, but Gloria and I enjoyed the parties afterward. With all our vacations completed, we returned to work on cases pending on each of our respective calendars.

On January 15, 1954, I tried the Kansas City, Missouri, municipal swimming pool case, to remove all racial restrictions on the use of pools owned and operated by the city. Blacks were admitted to all park facilities—including golf courses and theaters—but not swimming pool facilities. City authorities could point to no rule or regulation requiring the racial restriction and could only state that the restrictions seemed to be based on custom and usage. That did not hold up, and the court banned the practice. The lower court's ruling was affirmed on appeal.

During the mid-1950s our membership began seeking the institution of litigation by the legal staff to remove restrictions on the use of public golf courses, tennis courts, and other recreational facilities. While I was not opposed to opening these facilities to black people, it seemed to me that NAACP funds should finance only school cases, voting rights cases, and such. I agreed to draft the complaints and briefs and try the cases but insisted they be privately financed. On this basis several cases were instituted and won.

During the spring of 1954, Thurgood began to spend

extra time in Washington visiting the Supreme Court in the hope that he would be in the Court when it announced the decision in *Brown*. The Court usually recessed for the year sometime in June and always announced some decisions in the cases that had been argued that term. It was a good bet that we would have a decision in *Brown* in June at the latest. His diligence paid off. He was in the Court on May 17, 1954, when Chief Justice Warren announced the *Brown* decision.

Instead of immediate vindication, on May 31, 1955, in the *Brown* remedial decision the Court ordered enforcement over time "with all deliberate speed." With that decision I lost some of my reverence for the Supreme Court, realizing that black people could not rely on any white institution in this country to assert their rights, when such assertion was or appeared to be in conflict with a powerful competing white interest.

Until its decision in the *Gaines* case the Supreme Court had a dismal record of vindicating black rights under the Fourteenth Amendment. Indeed, except for voiding criminal convictions of black defendants by juries from which blacks had been eliminated by discrimination, the Fourteenth Amendment had not been accorded an expansive reading to guarantee equal citizenship rights for blacks. The privileges and immunities clause had been made inoperative, and the Fourteenth Amendment's reach was restricted to action by the states, so that the amendment could not be used to fight discrimination against blacks by individuals. Until the Franklin Delano Roosevelt administration came to power in 1932, the Court had largely interpreted the Fourteenth Amendment to expand corporate power and protect it from governmental restriction.

The Warren Court stands out for having interpreted the Fourteenth Amendment as a guaranty of equal educational opportunity for black people. Though the rights of the victorious litigant were never secured, since none of the plaintiffs in the South Carolina, Kansas, or Virginia cases ever attended an unsegregated school, the *Brown* decision revolutionized race relations in this country. What the *Brown* decision said to black people was that they were entitled to equality under the United States Constitution, and that they did not have to rely on the goodwill or largesse of whites to secure that right. This has made blacks more aggressive, more demanding—and race relations more volatile.

In my judgment the Court in *Brown II* sacrificed its integrity in a futile effort at appeasement. If immediate vindication had been ordered, the result would have been much the same as what occurred under the all-deliberate-speed mandate, but the Court's integrity would have been intact. Indeed, some eleven years later, tired of the lack of progress in eliminating the dual school system, the Court demanded immediate, concrete results.

For roughly a year after the decision it did look as if *Brown* would be accepted by the white community in the former Confederate states. The NAACP field staff worked with branches throughout the South in community action programs working for smooth acceptance of the decision. But by 1955, resistance to the decision had spread throughout the South. For the first time there were widespread threats of violence against the NAACP people in the southern states. Until *Brown* we had not been considered worthy of notice by the southern Bourbons, and our branches had been carrying out their local programs dedicated to fighting racial discrimination through community action and law with minor white resistance. That all changed after 1955.

## Chapter 6

# Fighting for Survival in the Wake of *Brown*

After *Brown* was decided, Thurgood, like the rest of us, was certain that the civil rights fight had been won and nothing more could be gained through the NAACP litigation program. He was ready now to seek a court appointment to the United States Court of Appeals, and began to make preparations for his succession. It quickly became clear, however, that the struggle had by no means ended.

In what was to become a widespread backlash against *Brown*, segregationists who had heretofore dismissed the NAACP as weak and powerless not only began to target our legal work, but threatened to destroy the NAACP itself and to bar it from functioning at the local, state, and national levels. Congressmen from the eleven former Confederate states took up the cry, calling for investigation of the organization and inquiry into its tax status.

Many segregationists believed that if the NAACP could be made dysfunctional, *Brown* would not be implemented. At this point the NAACP and its tax-exempt arm, the NAACP Legal Defense and Educational Fund (LDF), were in effect one intertwined organization.

Officers and board members held similar positions in both organizations. The threat of an inquiry into the LDF's tax status worried Thurgood. He consulted a tax lawyer at the firm of Paul, Weiss and thereafter structured the LDF as a freestanding entity, independent from the NAACP. Officers and board members could be affiliated with either the NAACP or the LDF, but not with both. When, in selecting the organization they would continue their affiliation with, all dual-membership-holding board members except Bill Hastie chose the NAACP over the LDF, Thurgood's ego was bruised. As Mr. Civil Rights and one of the most famed and esteemed African Americans in the country, he had expected them to follow him.

Without prior discussion I was summarily removed from the LDF, where I was Thurgood's chief deputy, and named general counsel of the NAACP, with Thurgood's assurance that nothing would change. I had worked for Thurgood for about twelve years, and one thing I knew about Marshall was that unless your work benefited him, you were of no interest to him, and it was highly unlikely that he would expend energy on your behalf. I was being discarded because he no longer felt he needed what I could offer. I was furious and not persuaded by his assurance that nothing would change. For one thing, I was no longer in line to succeed him. Although I had never consciously thought about being Thurgood's successor, being thus told by him that I was not going to inherit his job did not sit well with me.

I thought I deserved the courtesy of being told what was planned before being presented with a fait accompli. I felt betrayed and had a long litany of complaints. I had worked for him for twelve years, and through my creative vision, legal skills, and intellectual heft we had struck down the separate but equal doctrine in *Brown*, and officialdom could no longer order or maintain racial segregation or discrimination. Blacks were now equal to whites under law and did not have to rely on the goodwill of some white individual to reach that status. It was theirs by right. My vision and creative legal skills had produced these landmark race relations gains, and Thurgood had received all the credit without any complaint by me.

While I believe concern that the two groups had to be separated so that the LDF could continue to offer its donors tax exemption for their contributions was part of the motivation to separate the LDF from the NAACP, Thurgood also wanted to be his own boss. When Walter White had been the CEO, Thurgood had chafed under Walter's treatment. Thurgood's being a lawyer entitled him to no special status in White's view. He was the boss, and Thurgood was one of his employees. When a legal victory was achieved, Walter felt he had the right as the boss to first announce its implications in the organization program, and it was for him to say what the legal victory meant and where the organization was going with it.

What is not clear to me is why Walter did not talk to Thurgood before announcing what the favorable Court ruling the NAACP lawyers had won meant. The reasons

for Walter not seeking Thurgood's views and the fierce-
ness of Thurgood's anger and antipathy for his not doing
so are exceedingly complex, but the rivalry, jealousy, dis-
trust, and envy between Walter, Thurgood, and Roy
Wilkins were definite deterrents to understanding and
cooperation. Moreover, despite Walter's chutzpah and
ego, he must have been aware that the dominant power
base in the organization had shifted from him to Thurgood.

Thurgood and Roy, Walter's deputy, were allies,
united in a mutual distaste for Walter, and had conspired
to get rid of him. Both wanted Walter gone, Roy so that
he could become executive director of the NAACP,
Thurgood so that he would not be under a superior officer and could be his own boss. Nothing came of the various plots because Walter was a more skillful operator and
had access to more power within the NAACP and in the
larger world. In 1955, Walter conveniently died, allowing
Roy to become NAACP executive director and Thurgood to sever the LDF from the NAACP without opposition.

I did not know Walter very well although I had been
with the organization since 1944 and he had approved my
being hired. Thurgood encouraged me to think uncon-
ventionally, to concentrate on stretching the law to outlaw racial discrimination. He kept me out of office politics
and did not allow my ideas to be summarily dismissed in
discussions with our group of cooperating lawyers. My
contact with the office staff other than those working in
or for the legal department was minimal.

I had come to the NAACP with a master's degree in

law, giving me the credentials of a scholar. By that time it appeared that Thurgood had lost his zest and mental energy for legal research. He had become the most well known African American lawyer in the country and was now, in the public's eye, by far the dominant name in the NAACP. During his early years with the NAACP, Thurgood produced a series of landmark decisions outlawing segregation and discrimination in various areas of American life, including *Smith v. Allwright*, the 1944 decision that leveled the hurdles barring blacks from voting in Democratic Party primaries in the South. By the end of World War II, however, he had become more of a civil rights leader than a lawyer. He was, indeed, the public face of the association, traveling around the country, meeting with branches, drumming up support for the cause, and attempting to get change through community action in addition to litigation. He thrived in this role, which allowed him to use his extraordinary talents as a brilliant and charismatic leader.

He now needed someone on his staff to supply the intellectual weight and mental energy that he was no longer supplying. From the onset of our association I was the source of the energy and vision generating Court decisions affording black people equality under law, for which he received credit. That Thurgood was receiving credit was not an issue with me for a time. I was being given the opportunity to improve my lawyering skills and gain confidence that I could and would achieve my goal of becoming one of the best, if not the best, civil rights lawyers in the United States. The need for public recognition of my contributions to civil rights had not yet surfaced. Nevertheless, when I learned that I was to become general counsel of the NAACP, I realized that it was obviously a demotion. I was no longer in line to succeed Thurgood, and despite the high-sounding title, I had no staff, and it would require some creative energy and luck to provide substance to my new role. That requirement was temporarily postponed, since I was still working out of the LDF's offices and was handling all the pending cases over which I had exercised supervision and control as Thurgood's deputy.

Despite Thurgood's assurances that nothing would change, I knew otherwise. I was hurt and angry, believing that he had in effect kicked me in the head after all I had done for him in our professional relationship. For nearly a dozen years, I had done all the creative legal work for which he received credit, written all the major Supreme Court briefs for which he received credit, managed the office, and even written major articles in his name without any indication of my authorship; now it seemed to me that my reward was to be summarily pushed out.

My relationship with Thurgood had always been complicated, and was never a close, personal one. As his chief assistant, I was charged with doing and overseeing the legal work that the staff had to perform, and because of me, he did not have to be concerned about the quality of the legal work being done. He was free to indulge in long social lunches, and to tour the country to expand and invigorate our membership so that we could use community action, not just litigation, to achieve reforms.

I did not spend time laughing or joking with him during office hours or socializing with him after work. It was not that I did not like the man. He was engaging and had a great deal of earthy charisma. Nor was it because I was above doing the things one needs to do to flatter and please the boss even to the point of obsequiousness. We just did not mesh on a personal level. He liked to gamble, shoot dice, play poker for high stakes. I did not like to risk my money on high-stakes card games.

I liked to play the tamer, white bread games: poker with betting limits, hearts, pinochle, bridge. I liked opera and ballet; he preferred musicals. He was hearty, seemingly welcoming to all. I was reserved, selective, and introspective. Our differences were such that one wonders how we managed a relationship at all. I think it was because we never got in each other's way. We never scorned the other's tastes. Also, I was what Thurgood needed for about twelve years. When he came to believe that the NAACP had taken him as far as it could, he sought other options. I had no political insight to help him land the judicial or administrative appointments he had his eye on. My usefulness to him was over.

Thurgood's first wife, Buster, had become my ally early on. She approved of my role as Thurgood's deputy, and indeed, she may have urged him to give me that role. She was a very intelligent woman, very outgoing, and possessed a great deal of charm. She was devoted to her husband and used her influence to further his career. She saw in me one who would fulfill some of her husband's basic professional needs. She knew I was no threat to him. I did not have the personality for that. I was too shy. I could not stir a big crowd and had no such desire. I did not want to be a civil rights leader. Buster looked after me, and we developed a personal relationship. When she had people over for cards, she would have me join them. Buster became ill with cancer and died in 1955, coinciding with the rupture of my relationship with her husband. I have always thought that had Buster lived, my relationship with Thurgood might not have ended so badly, but I am no longer so certain.

Why my relationship with Thurgood soured so rapidly was not clear to me at the time, but what has become clear is the role played by Thurgood's LDF successor, Jack Greenberg. Jack, whom I regarded as a friend, made certain that I would not approach Thurgood for a talk or an explanation when our relationship ruptured in 1955. He stoked my anger, coming to me regularly to pass on some crude uncomplimentary remark he said Thurgood had made about me; I would in turn make an equally foul, denigrating remark about Thurgood. I don't know whether Thurgood ever told Jack the things he conveyed to me, and I never questioned then whether Jack was telling me the truth. Nor do I know whether Jack repeated my remarks to Thurgood. What Jack told me mirrored my feelings about Thurgood, and under the circumstances it was easy to believe what Jack told me had come from Thurgood.

It never occurred to me that in supposedly passing on Thurgood's hostile sentiments about me, Jack was furthering his own hidden agenda. I was too naive to ask myself, Why is this man coming to me with this stuff? If I had asked that question I would have seen that Jack had something in mind other than keeping me current on Thurgood's view of me. I was the preeminent civil rights lawyers' lawyer, highly regarded and respected among lawyers in the field. I had taken Jack on his first trial, and sat second seat to him and supervised him as he put on part of our direct case in *Brown v. Board of Education*, the rubric under which the school segregation cases from Kansas, South Carolina, and Virginia were argued and decided. With Louis Redding, an NAACP cooperating lawyer in Delaware, Jack tried two cases following the strategy and approach on the merits used in the *Brown* case, winning both.

I had no reason to regard Jack as an enemy until Thurgood left the LDF to accept an interim appointment on the Court of Appeals for the Second Circuit and Jack was named his successor. Almost immediately on becoming the LDF chief Jack the concerned friend became Jack the enemy who wanted to block me off from civil rights litigation. He wanted all such cases coming from the NAACP to be turned over to him, while I was to confine my legal activities to those of house counsel. Since I was not prepared to do that, we were in constant conflict. He conned Roy into supporting his agenda of handling civil rights litigation for the NAACP, and I was in constant conflict with Roy because of my no-holds-barred fight with Jack over this. Jack had the advantage of being able to deal with Roy one to one—the head of one organization dealing with the head of another.

Jack believed he could get Roy to support his plan and that Roy would order me to do what Jack wanted. Roy was unhappy with the harsh hostility that marked my dealings with Jack, but he never ordered me to turn over any cases to him. Roy knew that such an order would result in my open rebellion, and Roy always feared publicity unfavorable to the NAACP. Roy was not Walter, and early on I had told him that as the organization's lawyer, it was my responsibility to make the legal decisions and to decide on a legal program. He could have input, but mine was the final determination.

I was counsel of record in all the litigation that over the next several years was to result in significant U.S. Supreme Court civil rights decisions. At some point after Jack was named head of the LDF, I realized that he had betrayed what I believed was our friendship; he had played on my anger and hurt about what I regarded as Thurgood's betrayal to make sure the breach between Thurgood and me would not be bridged, thus ensuring that he would not have to compete with me for Thurgood's job at the LDF after Thurgood's wanted judgeship materialized.

Jack's betrayal was confirmed a few years after I had left the NAACP and become a partner in Poletti, Freidin, Prashker, Feldman & Gartner, a small, high-quality, and profitable commercial law firm. Jack and his first wife, Sima, were in the midst of bitter divorce proceedings. Sima was very bright and aggressive, and the type of woman who, if she felt wronged in the breakup of her marriage, was not going to go passively. I knew nothing about the pending divorce until out of the blue I received a call from Sima at my law firm. She told me that Jack had all the judges on his side, and she wanted them to know what an awful person he was and how shamefully she and the kids were being treated. "We know," she said, "what he did to you." She told me she believed there would be a better chance of her being believed if I would testify as her witness and tell the court how Jack had schemed against me to be sure he was named Thurgood's successor. I declined the invitation, telling her the court would probably regard my testimony as not relevant and not allow it. When I left the NAACP, my NAACP days were past me. I was attempting to master a new occupation—making money practicing law in a commercial law firm—and was not going to get involved in someone else's mess by airing dirty NAACP laundry.

I now realize my reaction to Thurgood's choice of successor was off the mark. Thurgood owed me nothing. He had paid me fully in allowing me to develop into a confident lawyer capable of more than holding my own in any appellate court in the country. I had successfully done some very creative things pushing against the edges of the law, for which he had received the credit, but I had been able and free to do them because he had taken all the responsibility on his shoulders. And in the process I had matured as a lawyer—had become a finished technocrat. I did not realize then, as I do now, that a boss really owes no loyalty to his assistants. He provides them with opportunity—in my case for growth in intellectual capacity and lawyering skills, and the opportunity to expand the parameters of legal jurisprudence in creative and imaginative ways. For that I owed him loyalty, but his obligations to me had been more than fulfilled. Still, even if I had been wise enough to see then what I see now, I doubt it would have had any immediate ameliorating effect.

The explanation for Thurgood's choice of successor would have been difficult for me to decipher at the time, and has only become clear to me as a result of my own subsequent experiences and reflections. Thurgood had this huge reputation as the foremost civil rights lawyer in the country, and his goal was to become a federal appellate judge. He had a shrewd sense of politics. He realized that his confirmation would face difficulties not only from the rabid segregationists but from more moderate senators as well. He thought, I'm virtually certain, that in choosing a white man to take his position, he was making clear that he would operate within an accepted race-relations format and hoped his choice would ease any fears of senators that he was a radical black man who would not judge white litigants fairly. Choosing a white man as his successor was not inevitable since there were a number of black lawyers certainly capable of succeeding Thurgood, such as Constance Baker Motley, from the NAACP's legal staff, and others who had worked with us—including Loren Miller, Robert Ming, Oliver Hill, and Spottswood Robinson.

The reason I believe this analysis has merit is because of what I experienced during confirmation of my appointment to the federal bench in Manhattan in 1972. The recurrent question asked was "Could you be fair to white people?" I was virtually unknown as a civil rights lawyer but had attracted widespread attention when I resigned from the NAACP in 1968 because Lewis Steel, a white member of my staff, had been fired without my being consulted. Four years later, at my confirmation hearing, Senator Everett Dirksen of Illinois, chairman of the Senate Judiciary Committee, wanted assurances that I could be fair to white litigants. The question annoyed me, though I was prudent enough to suppress the irritation in answering Senator Dirksen's inquiry in the affirmative.

Later, however, I saw no need to hold back the irritation when asked the same question in bar committee interviews; after responding yes, I asked whether white candidates were asked whether they could be fair to blacks, a much more pertinent question in my view, considering the history of brutal suppression and victimization of blacks by whites during and after slavery, plus data showing that white judges were consistently less generous toward black defendants than toward white defendants. I don't recall the responses, except that it caused my questioners some embarrassment. The reality is no white candidate is asked the question—his fairness is assumed, or else there is simply no concern about his being fair to blacks.

While my anger with Marshall's treatment of me was such that it completely undermined any relationship we had, I continued to do my professional job. In fact, in that sense, nothing had essentially changed. I handled the major cases as the NAACP fought for its life in the South in the aftermath of the *Brown* ruling. Instead of easing desegregation, the Supreme Court's 1955 "all deliberate speed" ruling in *Brown II* emboldened southern congressmen and state officials to call for defiance. A number of the segregating states reacted to *Brown* by threatening rebellion. In addition to the empty bombast, a number began targeting the NAACP for destruction by enacting new barratry statutes outlawing the NAACP method of encouraging people to institute litigation and undertaking their representation. Our lawyers who were members of the bars of Virginia, Alabama, and the states enacting these laws were under the threat of disbarment. Teachers were required to list their organizational connections, and known NAACP members were fired in many instances from their jobs. Many segregationists believed that getting rid of the NAACP would solve the problem. Without it, there would be no effort to implement the *Brown* decision.

The organization was under attack in almost all the eleven former Confederate states. Those states passed legislation redefining barratry to cover and outlaw the NAACP litigation strategy. Typically, for example, NAACP lawyers at the national level would announce that the organization was now prepared to sponsor litigation outlawing segregation in state colleges. The branches would be asked to recruit qualified applicants to apply for admission to a state college. When admission was refused, litigation would be instituted seeking a court order requiring admission to the college. The lawyers handling the litigation would be on the NAACP national staff of counsel hired by the national office. The organization would undertake a fund-raising drive on the basis of the litigation. Thus the NAACP conceived the action, secured the plaintiffs, provided the lawyers, prepared and filed the necessary court documents, and argued the matter before the court. A number of states, including Virginia, amended their barratry statutes to make this methodology illegal.

We decided in 1956 not to wait for an attack against us in Virginia but to attack first. Thurgood and I sought a declaratory judgment in the federal district court in Virginia to prevent enforcement of the law against the NAACP and the LDF on the grounds that the legislation was unconstitutional on its face and in its intended application to the two organizations. Since injunction of a state statute was being sought, the federal judge before whom the case was initially filed had to convene a three-judge court. While waiting for the case in Virginia to be set for hearing, I was faced with an immediate, more pressing problem. At about the same time Virginia enacted the statute we were testing, Attorney General John Patterson of Alabama secured an ex parte (meaning without our having been heard) temporary restraining order (TRO) from Judge Walter Jones—one of the state's corrupt and incompetent judges in Montgomery, Alabama—barring the NAACP from operating in the state.

If we were to be allowed to resume our activities, the attorney general of Alabama demanded that he be given a list of the names and addresses of all of our Alabama members. I went to Alabama immediately for a hearing on the TRO. I met with Ruby Hurley, our Southeast Regional secretary, whose jurisdiction included Alabama. Ruby was a very elegant woman with an engaging sense of style. A law school graduate, she was very smart, and one of the most competent and dedicated members on the NAACP staff.

The next morning I appeared in Judge Jones's courtroom with my witnesses, prepared to move that the TRO be dissolved on the grounds that the organization had a right to peacefully carry on its activities in the state. The attorney general contended that we were required to provide the names and addresses of our members as a precon-

dition to being heard. Judge Jones agreed and ordered me
to provide the state with the names and addresses of our
members by Monday next or we would be in contempt of
court and subject to a fine of $100,000.

I called Thurgood and told him I was flying back to
New York that night and needed to meet with him and
Roy the next morning, Saturday, in the LDF offices to
discuss the problem and decide how to handle it. Roy,
Thurgood, and I met that Saturday morning at about ten
o'clock. I was convinced to the point of a passionate belief
that we could not give the names and addresses of our
members to the state. To do so would expose our members to the threats of lost jobs, physical violence, even
possible loss of life, and would risk serious danger to their
families. Moreover, if we complied with the state's request, the organization would no longer be able to recruit
members in the state. It would be finished in Alabama. All
the black people would be afraid to join for fear their
names would be given to the local officials.

I was also certain that our activities, which involved
only peaceful protests and activity against racial discrimination imposed and enforced by the state, were protected
by the First Amendment. My research and knowledge on
the issue were not current, but having spent a year
(1940–41) in residence at Columbia University researching the First Amendment, I was reasonably confident that
I could bring our activities within its orbit. Thurgood was
adamant at first that we had to obey the court's order because our legal program relied on courts issuing orders in
our favor. We insisted that these orders be obeyed by others, and we could not now act as if we were above the law.

I told him our case was different. Jones was an ignorant segregationist and his order was arbitrary and capricious. It would not stand up on appeal. To risk the safety of our members by obeying an order issued by that incompetent man was the height of irresponsibility. Thurgood's problem was that he felt he had reached his ultimate goal as NAACP-LDF head counsel. He was looking beyond the NAACP and the LDF, using his political influence to secure a court appointment, and he did not want his record marred by being guilty of contumacious conduct.

I did not let up. I was determined to fight to the bitter end to secure approval to defy the order. I was so vigorously arguing for defiance as the only responsible course of action that Thurgood began to waiver. He decided to call Bill Hastie, and at the end of that conversation reported that Hastie had said we must obey the court's order. Although Hastie was still my idol, being told that he had said to obey the law did not persuade me to give up the fight. I also doubted that Thurgood had given an accurate summary of Hastie's views. Indeed, I was so committed to refusing to give up our membership list that if Hastie had been present and suggested that we obey Jones's order, I would have fought him.

Suddenly, Thurgood gave up the fight and said it was up to Roy to decide. His abdication was interesting because all three of us knew that Roy would do whatever Thurgood told him to do. Roy felt the situation was too critical for him to make a decision without consulting the board. He began telephoning board members, explaining the issues and what was at stake. Telephoning the board was not completed until early evening. What really struck me about the board members' responses was that every nonlawyer voted to defy the court order and risk paying the $100,000 fine and facing the contempt of court citation. On the other hand, and indicating how conservative lawyers are, almost all the lawyers voted to obey the court's order on the grounds that we could not afford to be in contempt of court because our legal program was built on obedience to court decisions. Their view was that we had to find some other way to deal with the consequences. When Roy reached the West Coast, Loren Miller, a lawyer, broke the pattern and said risk the fine. When the board's votes were counted, I was able to relax because a majority had voted for defiance.

The following Monday I was again in Montgomery before Judge Jones. I attempted to argue that he should give us the opportunity to be heard before issuing his order, but this argument was summarily denied. I then offered compliance with all of the order except giving the names and addresses of our members. He would not hear of that and found the NAACP in contempt, barred it from operating in the state, and fined it $100,000. He ended the hearing by stalking off the bench. For the first time ever I lost my head in a courtroom. As he was leaving the bench, I called him incompetent and corrupt, among other choice derogatory terms. This could have meant a personal citation for contempt, but he and Edmon L. Rhinehart were not interested in me. They had achieved their objective of shutting down the NAACP in the state, thus freeing them, they hoped, from efforts to eliminate racial segregation.

The brains behind the state's maneuvers, I am sure,

was Edmon L. Rhinehart, a young assistant attorney general of Alabama. He was a very smart segregationist, but his narrow focus on maintaining segregation caused him to use his smarts in a cheap and corrupt way, exercising executive and judicial power to deny us procedural due process. The state won a skirmish, and Rhinehart and Jones may have enjoyed a good laugh over cocktails and dinner, but the victory was founded on a false legal premise doomed to exposure unless we gave up, an unlikely prospect. That is the problem with people whose vision and mental reach are as restricted as segregationists': they may be bright and have good minds, as was certainly true of Rhinehart, but they have limited their views and thinking too narrowly to be able to see the wider canvas. The segregationists sought to maintain the status quo, but a change in race relations was inevitable—which white southerners should have known better than any other segment of our population.

I appealed Jones's order to the supreme court of Alabama by filing a petition for writ of certiorari, which prior decisions of the court had held to be the proper course in cases involving the type of constitutional issues in our case. However, in December 1956 the court dismissed the petition on the grounds that we should have sought relief by way of mandamus. There was no long delay in this initial decision because the court must have been confident that its decision would be the end of the matter. You cannot secure Supreme Court review of a decision of a state's highest court if the decision is based on adequate state grounds.

If we had chosen the wrong state procedure in seeking

review of the contempt order, as the Alabama Supreme Court indicated, the U.S. Supreme Court would not review our claim, and I would have made a damaging mistake. Fortunately, Justice Black was well versed in Alabama procedure and wrote the opinion granting our petition for review by the high court. He held that Alabama precedent showed certiorari was the proper course, contrary to the state court's December 1956 dismissal.

I was as agitated as Frank Williams had been in the *Watts* case about whether Thurgood was going to take over the argument. The LDF and the NAACP were supposedly independent entities, so Thurgood had no jurisdiction over me. In fact he was operating as if the LDF were the tax-exempt arm of the NAACP and he was head counsel of both. He had no intention of not letting me argue the case. First Amendment jurisprudence was a subject he was not interested in, and as NAACP general counsel, it was properly my responsibility to make the Supreme Court presentation. Yet I could not be certain until it was made clear that the case was mine. So when discussing the issues with Thurgood and other lawyers, I used my greater knowledge of First Amendment jurisprudence. I attempted to make the issues so complex and a firm grasp of First Amendment jurisprudence so essential to success that it would dampen any interest he might have in taking the case and bolster my chances of being allowed to make the Supreme Court argument. I could have spared myself all the worry and energy.

This case (*NAACP v. Alabama*) was my first time appearing before the Court independent of Thurgood; I don't remember him even being in the courtroom. I argued that our rank-and-file members had the protection of the First Amendment to band together to agitate peacefully for the elimination of segregation and other forms of racial discrimination. This right, I argued, could be theirs only if they could do so anonymously, given the very real possibility of threats, and economic and physical reprisals, if their identities were revealed to the state.

Justice John Marshall Harlan, whose grandfather had filed the only dissent in *Plessy v. Ferguson*, was a new member of the Court. He wrote the opinion holding that as long as the officers of the NAACP in Alabama were revealed, the rank-and-file members of the organization had the right to assemble anonymously to agitate peacefully through the NAACP against racial discrimination. This was a great victory, but enforcement took years. The case was sent back to the Alabama Supreme Court, which did nothing for a while. Then it again dismissed the case, this time on the ground that we had failed to meet some other conditions.

We took this back to the Supreme Court, which rejected this holding on the ground that the case had been presented by both parties on one set of issues and the Court opinion was based on those issues. It was now too late to raise new ones. The supreme court of Alabama just let the matter sit without taking any action. Finally, I filed suit in the federal court to have it issue the necessary order allowing resumption of our activities in the state. The federal litigation succeeded in bypassing the state court's stalling tactics, and in 1964 the NAACP was finally able to resume operations in Alabama. The lesson here is that court decisions can be and are at times defied by lower courts.

When *Brown* was decided I realized that black teachers would be vulnerable, so I made a project of researching the laws of the states where the dual school system was mandatory and those where it was permissive. A group of highly qualified black teachers was fired in Moberly, Missouri, with the dismantling of the dual school system. All white teachers, even the most inexperienced with minimum qualifications, were retained, and new white teachers were hired. At the trial the superintendent testified that all the white teachers were superior to the black ones. He dismissed the objective standards showing higher qualifications in terms of graduate degrees and more experience as teachers. The trial court ruled against us. I secured the permission of all but one of the teachers to file an appeal. We lost on appeal, and the Supreme Court refused review.

This was a very serious setback. If school superintendents were free to disregard objective criteria and evaluate black and white teachers solely on the basis of a subjective racist standard, black teachers were subject to wholesale dismissals. With their livelihood in jeopardy they could not be expected to welcome the implementation of *Brown* in their school districts. I do not know why the problem I feared did not develop. Perhaps the slow pace of *Brown*'s enforcement in the South was a factor, and maybe teacher shortage was another. If the wholesale firing I feared had occurred and been allowed to stand on the basis of a racist subjective standard, there would have been a national scandal forcing the Supreme Court to face the issue. Subjective standards may prevail in the selection of key personnel, but to have them prevail with run-of-the-mill employees is absurd. In any event, disaster was averted, and, surprisingly, black teachers were enthusiastic in support of *Brown*.

In 1957, following the examples of Alabama and Virginia, Louisiana, Texas, Arkansas, Florida, and Georgia enacted anti-NAACP laws, and fifteen cities in Arkansas enacted local ordinances requiring local NAACP branches there to submit the names and addresses of their members to city authorities. I urged our local branches to keep the heat on by agitating for the removal of all forms of racial restrictions on the use of all public facilities—schools, public transportation, recreational facilities, public housing, and other forms of governmental services operated on a racially discriminatory basis. If community pressure and agitation did not work, the branches must come to the national office and seek litigation. We had to deal with these attacks on the organization, but we could not let them slow down or delay our drive for our main priority, which was the elimination of all forms of racial discrimination in the country.

In 1957 we instituted *NAACP v. Patty* seeking a declaratory judgment that new Virginia statutes that defined barratry as financing litigation and supplying counsel for litigants were an unconstitutional interference with NAACP peaceful protest activities under the Fourteenth Amendment's equal protection guarantee. This case, which became *NAACP v. Button*, was ultimately decided in our favor in 1964. We were banned in Louisiana in 1956 and not restored until we were able to secure a favorable ruling by the Supreme Court in February 1960.

Arkansas brought suit against the NAACP for not paying corporate franchise taxes. In addition it enacted legislation requiring all public-school teachers to list their organizational affiliations as a condition of employment. In a closely divided Court in *Shelton v. Tucker*, we succeeded in having the legislation outlawed. We continued to have trouble in Arkansas, but Daisy Bates and her husband were veteran NAACP fighters. They published a weekly newspaper and since the 1940s had quite courageously opposed racial discrimination. They continued taking courageous positions against racial discrimination and segregation. We fought efforts to silence Daisy Bates and secured a Supreme Court ruling providing protection for her and her publication under the Fourteenth Amendment's free speech guarantee.

By the end of 1957 we were involved in twenty-five cases seeking our membership list, defining our activities under new legislation as barratry. Increasingly, the states also began using a legislative-investigative-committee tactic, purportedly seeking information about our activities. This was a skillful technique to terrorize our unsophisticated members. Florida and Virginia initiated this kind of proceeding. We hoped that we would be able to neutralize these tactics because Supreme Court precedent held that this form of state power was not without limitation. In *Watkins v. United States* and in *Sweezy v. New Hampshire* the Court had held in situations markedly like our own that constitutional guarantees of liberty and due process protected the individual against abuse by state and federal legislative branches as well as against judicial deprivation.

In 1958, the Court in *Bates v. Little Rock* struck down a city ordinance requiring the production of our membership list. In other states, however, the authorities continued to press for our membership list. They began using another weapon, instituting criminal proceedings against our branch presidents and other officers for refusing to produce the lists. If successful, such proceedings could result in prison terms of up to six months. In *Gremillion v. NAACP* both the lower federal and appeals courts struck down a statute requiring the organization to provide the names and addresses of its members and to file an affidavit that none of its national officers were members of any subversive group. Surprisingly, the Supreme Court granted review. In view of its decisions in *NAACP v. Alabama* and *Bates v. Little Rock*, it had been expected that the Court would affirm the lower courts' decisions without hearing oral argument, and the fact that it did not had me worried. The case was argued on April 26, 1961, and the Court reached the same conclusion it had in the two previous cases.

In December of 1959, Thurgood moved to complete my separation from the LDF. At the time, I was preparing for extended travel in Europe. The trip was partly professional and partly personal. I was to give a lecture on American constitutional law in Rome to the Society for African Culture. Gloria and I combined this with a winter holiday in London, Paris, Florence, Rome, and Taormina, Sicily, before returning to New York. As I was leaving the office, Thurgood gave me his best wishes for a pleasant trip and handed me a letter that he said I should not read until after completing my flight to London.

I disregarded his instructions and opened the letter as soon as Gloria and I had settled in our seats. In the letter, he told me that on my return I should move to the NAACP offices at 20 West Fortieth Street. This meant moving from the proximity of other lawyers to NAACP headquarters, where I would be the only attorney in residence. In my mind this completed the kicking-out process, but it at least made sense that as the organization attorney, I would have my office on its premises. Being physically off the LDF's premises would make clear that my close relationship with Marshall had changed, that we were not bound together as we had been.

I believe now that Thurgood may have hoped I would take my removal from his staff like a good trouper. Instead I reacted in anger and hurt. While we never said one harsh word directly to each other, my anger and feeling that he had badly used me were no secret, and our relationship— after a rewarding professional collaboration spanning nearly a dozen years—had deteriorated badly by that day in December 1959 when my wife and I flew to London. When we returned from Europe in January 1960, I moved out of the LDF offices to NAACP national headquarters at 20 West Fortieth Street. There I continued to work on the major civil rights cases that I was responsible for as Thurgood's deputy, and for which I was the attorney of record. That year I also began work on a major voting rights case that had come through the branches.

While I was Thurgood's deputy the legal department

had held lawyers' conferences at each annual convention. At these conferences lawyers who worked with the local branches attended, and we would agree on a proposed national legal program for the year. I would tell the branch lawyers what I proposed for the national staff legal program, suggest that they adopt it locally, and advise the delegates on how to deal with legal issues that they wanted to attack in their communities. These conferences usually inspired very spirited discussions. They did not simply involve national staff dispensing wisdom. Blacks were beginning in sizable numbers to attend first-rate law schools. Thus a cadre of well-trained lawyers affiliated with the NAACP began to grow. At each conference we sought to come away with a consensus on what the national office and the branches' legal activities would be, and with varying degrees of success we managed to do that.

I continued to hold these conferences as NAACP general counsel, and at our convention in Dallas, I was holding the lawyers' conference when Fred Gray of Montgomery, Alabama, came to me with the draft of a brief seeking appellate review of *Gomillion v. Lightfoot*, a case that he had tried and lost. He had been engaged by the Tuskegee NAACP branch to litigate the gerrymander of the city. White authorities had undertaken to place all blacks outside the city limits and thereby prevent their voting in any local election. Because blacks lived all over the city and were not confined to one area, the gerrymander was a crazy, weaving line—up, down, back and forth—eliminating all but one or two black voters from the city's rolls. After concluding the lawyers' conference, I read Fred's draft and agreed to help. With his consent I took charge of the matter, writing the petition for Supreme Court review and the brief on the merits, and arguing the case before the Supreme Court with Fred.

*Gomillion* was presented as a voters' rights case—blacks were being denied their Fifteenth Amendment right to vote by being cast off the voter rolls through the gerry-mander. That Justice Frankfurter wrote the opinion de-claring the gerrymander an unconstitutional denial of the voting rights of black residents of Tuskegee was of great significance. Frankfurter had been a leading advocate of judicial abstinence when confronted with controversies over the drawing or revising of political districts, but he accepted our argument that here the gerrymander posed a Fifteenth Amendment voters' rights controversy that the Court could and should resolve. Once *Gomillion* was decided, a series of one-man-one-vote decisions fol-lowed—including *Raymond v. Sims* and *Baker v. Carr.* An article about *Gomillion* appeared in the *New Yorker* soon after the decision.

The Court set *NAACP v. Patty* down for reargument in its next term, beginning October 1962. I do not recall much of the reargument except that it must have been without difficulty. In any event, on January 14, 1963, the Court issued its holding in the case (now called *NAACP v. Button*), which was a very vital civil rights victory. *Button* provided First Amendment protection for the activities of organizations such as the NAACP that engage in protest activities through the court process—those that use court litigation to fight racial or other forms of discrimination. This meant that we and other organizations could now freely conceive litigation to attack various forms of discrimination, recruit plaintiffs, finance the litigation, hire the lawyers, write the briefs, and argue the issues before the courts. Lawyers could now operate as Charles Houston had conceived, as social engineers.

*Chapter 7*

# Taking *Brown* North

*Brown v. Board of Education* recast the civil rights movement, but the transformation took time in manifesting itself. *Brown* established coequal citizenship rights for all Americans without differentiation based on race, color, or ethnicity. The protests that followed in the aftermath of *Brown* put the nation on notice that blacks would fight for and defend their equality. Direct action became the new device. Young people, impatient with the pace of change, formed the Student Nonviolent Coordinating Committee in 1960 and transformed direct action into something of an art form of protest—freedom rides, sit-ins, kneel-ins, anything that would bring discomfort to public officials seeking to uphold racial discrimination. Black protest, which reached new heights in the South, now intensified in the North as well, spreading throughout the whole country.

Simultaneously, the election of John F. Kennedy as president in 1960 seemed to usher in a new era, marking the passing of leadership to the generation of soldiers who had fought in World War II. Kennedy came to the White House with no strong views about civil rights or providing equal rights for blacks. Once he took office, however, he became the focus of a drive for equal rights and justice for black Americans, and by 1963 he found himself and his party proposing sweeping civil rights legislation. Under Lyndon Johnson's leadership, the Civil Rights Act of 1964 was the most comprehensive legislation of its kind to be enacted into law in this country.

As long as Thurgood was at the helm of the Legal Defense Fund, the relationship between the LDF and the NAACP continued along the lines that had previously been established so far as litigation was concerned. Thurgood attended the association's annual meeting and met with NAACP lawyers to discuss cases and strategies. He was regarded by everyone as the premier civil rights attorney in the country, as well as the main lawyer for our branches. When I moved to West Fortieth Street in 1960, I took the cases I was working on with me, which included challenges arising from efforts to implement *Brown*, the string of cases fighting for the right of the NAACP to exist in the South, and the *Gomillion* case.

My tenure as NAACP general counsel was almost cut short in 1961. That summer, the *New York Times* reported that I would be nominated for appointment to the federal District Court for the Southern District of New York (Manhattan). I had friends close to the administration, including Louis Harris, the noted pollster, and Justin Feld-

man, a powerful New York attorney and my former classmate at Columbia Law School. They promoted my name
among administration officials who were anxious to appoint a black person to the federal bench. Kennedy had
initially offered a district judgeship to Thurgood, but he
turned it down; he would settle for nothing less than an
appointment to the court of appeals. At this point, Kennedy was not prepared to reward a black with such a pres-
tigious post.

The *New York Times* published a front-page story that I
was to be appointed to the federal bench in Manhattan. I
had not worked in Democratic Party politics in New
York, and the local lords were not happy that an appointment of such high prestige was to go to someone who had
not paid his dues. I was not known publicly, as was Thurgood. Only lawyers working with the NAACP or closely
connected to it knew that much of the credit Thurgood
had received as Mr. Civil Rights since *Smith v. Allwright*
stemmed from Supreme Court decisions based on my
work. Louis Martin, a seasoned black political operator
who was seeking to help get as many blacks appointed to
high-level posts as possible, advised me to secure Congressman Adam Clayton Powell's endorsement. I visited
Powell in his office on Capitol Hill. He made it clear that
his support would cost $20,000. I reported this to my
friends, who relayed it to the Kennedys, who in turn confronted Powell. However, they needed Powell, the powerful chair of the House Committee on Labor and
Education, more than they needed me. My prospective
nomination was dropped, and Marshall's desire for a place
on the court of appeals became the better alternative.

Thurgood was nominated to the court of appeals on September 23, 1961. Four days later the LDF executive committee agreed on Jack Greenberg as Thurgood's successor, and presented this to their board on October 4, 1961. A press release announcing the selection of Jack was issued that same afternoon, prior to any notification of or consultation with the NAACP's board. The story that ran in the press suggested that there were two names before the LDF board—Jack's and mine—which was incorrect. I was not a candidate for the LDF directorship. The *New York Times* article announcing Jack's selection made no distinction between the two organizations and referred to Jack as the NAACP's general counsel.

As the new director of the LDF, Jack Greenberg sought to have me confined to handling only organizational issues and no civil rights litigation whatsoever. Obviously this did not go down well with me. I had been a creator of the civil rights litigation the NAACP and the LDF had engaged in up to the separation of the two organizations. As NAACP general counsel I had under my control all the pending civil rights litigation of the LDF and the NAACP and several cases I had prepared for immediate filing.

It was obvious that in the aftermath of Thurgood's departure from the LDF, the nature of the relationship between the LDF and the NAACP had to be clearly defined. I proposed that the NAACP do one of two things: either order Jack Greenberg and his group to become part of the NAACP's legal arm, or, if that wasn't possible, prevent them from using the NAACP initials. Roy was worried: he didn't know what to do, and he was getting conflicting advice. I later learned that Bob Ming, who sat on both the LDF and the NAACP boards, led a powerful clique on the NAACP board that blocked any effort to follow through on what I suggested. Most people, I believe, didn't understand what was going on and were suspicious of my involvement. In their view, my objections arose from personal ambition and reflected a sour grapes attitude because I had not been chosen to replace Thurgood. Unfortunately, Bob Ming was able to convince the NAACP board that this was the case, which served to immobilize them. Roy didn't see what the issues were until it was too late. I think he was more concerned about who might come out ahead and chose to let matters stay as they were.

The Legal Defense Fund purported to be the legal arm of the NAACP, even though now it was a completely separate entity. Jack Greenberg wanted to take all of the civil rights cases generated by NAACP branches and relegate me as NAACP chief lawyer to the internal work inherent to a corporate entity. I did not see any future for me if that was to be the division of labor. More important, I felt that no outside organization should take over the legal work of our branches. It had been through the activity of the NAACP branches that people had been moved to seek their rights and embark on litigation. The ongoing civil rights struggle required that the NAACP maintain its original structure in which the legal department functioned over a wide range of civil rights cases, in coordination with a membership prepared to generate and support such activity.

The LDF was focused on school desegregation in the

South, and I decided not to fight them on that territory. *Brown* had settled the legal issue with regard to school segregation in the South; now enforcement was the primary challenge. By 1961, I had already begun to concentrate on the problem of school segregation and inferior education outside of the South. Although not mandated by law, it was a fact of life for the great majority of black children. This was one of the most frightening issues facing blacks in northern urban areas and offered fertile ground for developing and expanding the interpretation of the *Brown* mandate. Northern branches were becoming more insistent that the national office lend greater leadership to the fight against racial discrimination in their communities. As I wrote Roy in a 1959 memo, the problem of school segregation in the North was a field in which our resources would do more than any other single issue to solidify support for the NAACP.

I began building a small legal staff, and hired Maria Marcus and Barbara Morris. On my urging, Roy appointed June Shagaloff as the NAACP's first special assistant for education. June, a white woman of Russian-Jewish descent, had worked with the NAACP since the early 1950s as a field worker. Trained as a social scientist, June had investigated school conditions in border and northern cities, and worked with local branches to challenge discriminatory policies and practices. She brought a wealth of experience and a deep commitment to ending school segregation in all of its guises.

June and I issued a coast-to-coast call to action, working with the Department of Branches to launch a challenge to northern-style school segregation. In response to a request from NAACP branches in California, we began with a tour of the West Coast to provide guidance in the implementation of a school desegregation program. We asked branches to make inventories of their communities, investigating school conditions and zoning patterns, and to determine whether integration might be accomplished by rezoning or other methods of reorganization. In our travels across the country, we met with state and local education officials and tried to persuade them to desegregate their schools, providing them with ideas and suggestions on how they might reorganize their school systems. All the while, we coordinated our efforts with our extensive network of NAACP branches. I was continually working to get our branches involved in efforts to make *Brown* a reality in this country, and they responded with great enthusiasm. Local branches assisted in factfinding and consulted with me for guidance with respect to effective community action as well as possible litigation strategies.

Our investigation of school systems outside of the South revealed, as June reported, that in nearly every case considerations of color alone, to the extent that housing segregation permitted, determined the basic organization of the public school system. While schools located at the center of large urban areas were segregated due exclusively to housing patterns, predominantly white and black schools in fringe areas of cities and suburban communities often reflected an intent to maintain racially separate schools. Regardless of whether segregation was intended or not, our investigation made clear that racially segregated public schools resulted in lowered educational standards and inferior opportunities in schools that serviced black children. Separate and unequal were found to go hand in hand, no less in the North than in the South.

The problem was vast and mirrored the kind of challenge Charles Houston had faced nearly three decades earlier when he embarked on the campaign to defeat Jim Crow. It required a multifront battle that joined local organizing and public agitation with an imaginative use of the law and social science in an effort to break new ground. Community action was a major theme. Branches across the country petitioned school boards, attempted to work with local school officials, staged boycotts, and mounted mass protests in an NAACP-led effort to desegregate public schools in the North and West.

June and I developed a number of models and plans responsive to the varied circumstances in small and large communities, and presented them to school boards around the country. They included rezoning to cut across black and white neighborhood schools; the Princeton plan, or paired schools, which assigned students by grade to two or three schools in a single attendance area; eliminating permissive transfers, which enabled white students to avoid attending predominantly black schools; closing segregated schools and reassigning teachers and students to existing schools; and selecting school sites to achieve desegregation. By the start of the 1962–63 school year a few gains had been made. A dozen school districts had adopted districtwide plans to either end or significantly reduce segregation, using a variety of approaches. But resistance was strong, and few northern communities were willing to admit that there was a problem requiring government action or intervention.

In June 1963, the Boston School Committee rebuffed the efforts of Ruth Batson, chair of Boston's NAACP education committee, to bring the concerns of black parents before the committee, and refused even to acknowledge that de facto segregation characterized Boston's public schools. That fall, June, Ruth Batson, Tom Atkins—head of the Boston branch's legal committee—and I met with representatives of the Massachusetts Civil Rights Commission and the Massachusetts Commission of Education to address the problem of school segregation in the city and devise a strategy for compelling school and public officials to reorganize school attendance patterns. Thus began the long struggle in that city that culminated with a court-ordered busing plan a decade later.

Segregation, whites in most northern communities contended, was a southern problem. According to the dominant line of reasoning, racial separation in the North, if it existed, was accidental, and therefore beyond the reach of the Fourteenth Amendment. Northern officials preferred terms like "racial imbalance" to describe the demographic profile of most northern school systems or de facto segregation as distinguished from segregation mandated by law, which came to be referred to as de jure segregation. It gave the impression that the deleterious impact on the black child, accepted as a causal result of de jure segregation, was nonexistent or, at most, minimal.

As the issue of northern school segregation gained more visibility, white parents and school officials seized on the concept of the neighborhood school as justification for the maintenance of the status quo. The ideal of the neighborhood school became the rallying point, an image of what once was but rarely existed in the highly urbanized and mobile culture of the 1960s. While the common school of the past was designed to serve a heterogeneous community, rigid adherence to this concept in the early sixties served principally to separate children by race and class, keeping black children separate and apart. Almost invariably, black children attended schools of low quality and academic disrepute, schools no one would choose to go to. The neighborhood school was rapidly becoming a euphemism for northern segregation.

There was a growing awareness of the problem of segregation in northern schools, and significant support for our position. The New York State Board of Regents and the California State Board of Education issued statements acknowledging that racial segregation perpetuated unequal education, and advised local school boards to work affirmatively through zoning and site selection to further integration. The great majority of six hundred educators surveyed by the American Education Association said that racial imbalance had a strong adverse effect on the black child's educational motivation. The commissioners of education in New York and New Jersey ruled that racial imbalance impaired educational opportunity and lowered the black child's motivation to learn. In 1965 the Massachusetts legislature passed the Racial Imbalance Act, requiring school committees to implement desegregation plans wherever schools were more than fifty percent black.

These pronouncements and laws provided important guideposts, but white resistance and the refusal of many communities to abide by such mandates obstructed effective enforcement in most cases. We sought and needed a definitive court interpretation of the due process and equal protection clause of the Fourteenth Amendment that would require the elimination of de facto segregation in the nation's public schools. In *Brown* the Supreme Court had stressed the fact that the separation of black children from others of similar age and qualifications solely because of race generated a feeling of inferiority in a way unlikely ever to be undone. Segregation was found to have a detrimental effect, and the impact was even greater when it had the sanction of law. The implication of the court's ruling, then, was that some disadvantage occurred whenever separation existed, while the evil was greater when required by law. Thus, if segregated education was inferior education constitutionally, there must be a constitutional requirement imposed on school authorities to take every step possible to eliminate or alleviate segregation.

We felt the only way for a school board to determine whether its schools were divided into black and white schools was to take a race census. We would then use the results to achieve as many integrated schools as possible. We were met with a great deal of criticism; people argued that if we were trying to build a color-blind society, then to use race as a criterion was moving backward. Some of these people may have been sincere—but most were hypocrites, with no interest in breaking down existing racial barriers.

Our proposal met fierce opposition. With their stereo-typical view of blacks, some white people believed their children would be deprived of quality education if required to attend schools where many black children attended. I was shocked at the vehemence of white resistance. Whites were prepared to call for Alabama, Georgia, and other southern communities to provide equal educational opportunity for blacks, but the schools their children attended were off limits.

By 1964, we had made some headway, although the court rulings were mixed concerning the validity of de facto segregation and the legality of laws designed to eliminate it. We brought court litigation in some dozen cities, including Cleveland; Milwaukee; Gary, Indiana; Denver; Pasadena, California; Springfield, Massachusetts; East Orange, New Jersey; and Manhasset, New York. A series of rulings in several cities held that de facto segregation violated the Constitution or was educationally undesirable, and ordered that the respective school boards develop desegregation plans. *Blocker v. Board of Education of Manhasset* (1964) provided the best judicial analysis affirming the right of black children not to be segregated, but the ruling was so narrowly drawn that it had no application elsewhere.

In other cases, most notably *Bell v. School City of Gary, Indiana*, the courts ruled that school officials were not in violation of the law if school lines were not deliberately drawn to perpetuate segregation. Furthermore, *Bell* held that any attempt to effectuate multiracial schools that involved procedures using race as a criterion were illegal. Ultimately, as I advised the branches, until the U.S.

Supreme Court decided the issue, we had to press forward with the view that de facto school segregation was educationally and legally indefensible, and that school authorities were required to take corrective action wherever school segregation existed in fact. As I recall, de facto segregation as a way to describe northern school segregation surfaced for the first time in the *Bell* case.

While we sought to break new ground in the struggle for educational equity and school desegregation in the North, the NAACP was fighting for its survival in the South. From 1955 on, state officials throughout the South engaged in a relentless campaign to cripple the organization and destroy its effectiveness. State legislatures and local officials tested a variety of tactics, enacting statutes effectively barring NAACP lawyers from operating in certain states, empowering state investigative agencies to secure membership lists, forbidding teachers and other public employees from participating in the NAACP, indicting individual leaders on trumped-up charges, and other methods. By 1964, civil suits for damages suffered as a result of picketing had become another weapon of harassment.

In defending itself, its members, its contributors, and its lawyers from these repressive governmental regulations and actions, the NAACP was thrust into the broad field of civil liberties. If a legal basis for destroying the NAACP was found, any organized effort by blacks to secure equality would be severely hampered. By the early 1960s, the importance of the sit-ins and the direct-action protests had been recognized, for it placed blacks in a new posture of open defiance. Yet the significance of anti-

NAACP legislation and litigation was not so clearly understood, particularly as it related to the survival of the movement. This struggle, I believed, was of far greater consequence to the resolution of the fight for equal citizenship than the completion of token integration of southern schools, for it was a fundamental matter of individual liberty to participate in lawful group activity to secure equal rights for blacks. While it taxed the resources of our small legal office, it was a fight that had to be continually engaged.

While *NAACP v. Alabama* had given First Amendment protection to the activities of the organization and its members, the South did not give up the campaign to stifle our activities and enfeeble the NAACP. The Florida legislature, in a supposed inquiry into activities of the group, subpoenaed the president of the Miami branch to appear before its committee and bring the membership lists of the branch to the hearing for disclosure to the legislative committee. He refused and was threatened with incarceration. We brought suit, and in *Gibson v. Florida* (1963) the court struck down this attempted end run around our First Amendment protection, declaring that Florida's Legislative Investigative Committee was a forbidden interference with the First Amendment rights of our members in that state.

Our branch in Savannah picketed a store in the black community that refused to hire black clerks and called for a boycott by the black community. The store sued for damages and recovered a fairly large amount of money. The lower courts' decisions in this case were upheld by the Supreme Court in *NAACP v. Overstreet.*

We scored another major Supreme Court victory in 1964 when the Court ordered the reopening of the public schools in Prince Edward County, Virginia, where black children had been without public education for eight years. In a 6–2 ruling the Court approved our argument that the state could not, on racial grounds, continue to deprive children in Prince Edward County of the opportunity to attend public school while providing the opportunity in other counties. In *Griffin v. County School Board of Prince Edward County*, the Court held:

> The record in the present case could not be clearer that Prince Edward's public schools were closed and private schools operated in their place with state and county assistance, for one reason and one reason only: to insure, through measures taken by county and state, that white and colored children in Prince Edward County would not, under any circumstances, go to the same school. Whatever nonracial grounds might support a state's allowing a county to abandon public schools, the object must be a constitutional one, and grounds of race and opposition to desegregation do not qualify as constitutional.

The Court stated with finality: "The time for mere deliberate speed has run out."

During these years, we kept up the fight against employment discrimination. In 1964 we secured a major victory when the National Labor Relations Board ruled that racial discrimination by a labor union was an unfair labor practice. The case involved the Independent Metal

Workers Union, which represented workers of the Hughes Tool Company. Production and maintenance employees at Hughes Tool were organized into two unions—one white, one black. The two unions were jointly certified as bargaining representatives of the company's employees. The white local negotiated an extension of the collective bargaining agreement reserving certain jobs for whites, despite the protest and refusal of the black union to execute the agreement. With the discriminatory agreement in place, the company refused to allow a black employee an apprenticeship on a "white" job. The white local refused to process the black employee's grievance. I filed an unfair labor practice charge on behalf of the black local with the NLRB and moved to have the NLRB rescind the white union's certification. The NRLB held that a union acting as the exclusive bargaining representative must represent all employees in the bargaining unit fairly without discrimination and that a labor organization organized into racially segregated units could not secure NLRB certification. Those heretofore certified were subject to decertification. The decision was handed down by Howard Jenkins, the first African American to serve on the NLRB and was announced on July 2, 1964, the day that President Lyndon Johnson signed the Civil Rights Act.

The passage of the Civil Rights Act of 1964 put the power of the federal government behind the promise of legal equality inherent in *Brown v. Board* not only in education but also in employment and all phases of public life. After the NAACP's annual meeting in Washington, D.C., that summer, I joined a small group of NAACP activists, mostly members of various NAACP branches in the northeast, and traveled to Mississippi to test the enforcement of the law with regard to public accommodations. Eugene Reed, president of the New York State NAACP, led the group. Reporters from the *New York Times*, the Associated Press, the *Chicago Sun*, and a couple of other news media joined us on the trip.

Although personal harm to any of us was unlikely, we were not free from some anxiety. We visited Canton and Jackson, staying in previously segregated hotels and eating in newly integrated restaurants. The one holdout we encountered was Philadelphia, Mississippi, the place where James Cheney, Andrew Goodman, and Michael Schwerner had gone missing a month earlier. Officials there refused to yield to the federal civil rights law, insisting that segregation would still be enforced. Our efforts to visit the area where the burned station wagon of the three civil rights workers had been found were rebuffed by county attorney Rayford Jones. In a tense exchange, I took exception to Jones calling me by my first name. He answered, "Now, Robert, you are here and you'll do things our way, and I'll call you what I want." I responded, in what was to some a shocking affront to white southern etiquette, "If that's the way you want to do it, Rayford, that's the way it will be."

While there were pockets of resistance, the Civil Rights Act, followed by the Voting Rights Act a year later, had a great impact on the South, striking down the legal structures that had confined black lives and opportunities and dictated race relations in the region for more than half a century. By the mid-1960s, peaceful black protests and violent white resistance had focused national attention on the South and helped mobilize sentiment in behalf of dismantling America's homegrown apartheid system. White northerners looked upon the crude and open racism of the South with horror. It had become a national and international embarrassment. President Lyndon Johnson proved brilliantly adept at marshaling national support for the most far-reaching civil rights legislation since the Reconstruction era.

Even before the passage of the civil rights legislation of the mid-1960s, the terrain of black protest and race relations in the United States was undergoing a profound change. While Martin Luther King Jr. was preaching love to southern blacks, black nationalists, Muslims, and blacks in neither category were expressing frustration and bitterness with the virulent racial discrimination that was part of every northern community. Most white northerners responded with discomfort and dismay to the torrent of antiwhite sentiment that bubbled to the surface. However, the blunt truth was that discrimination had been accepted if not condoned throughout the United States. In the North, despite its civil rights laws and antidiscrimination statutes, black people were not supposed to expect equal pay, equal education, equal housing, equal anything. Black life in the urban North underscored the gulf that persisted between what the law said a black person's status was and his position in fact.

Antiwhite sentiment was being voiced daily loudly and clearly. It had become an accepted posture in the black community, so that black lawyers took it to the courtroom, not rising when the judge entered. Black lawyers would turn their backs on the judge, addressing their remarks to the courtroom spectators. This open show of black disaffection ran its course. There was a superficial change in the race-relations arena. Blacks were treated courteously by white merchants. America began to look like a multiracial society, with people of color in evidence at every level of the society except at its highest reaches. A few successes were made even there.

While the media and liberal spokesmen heralded each step toward equal justice and opportunity as if the battle had been won, for most blacks very little change had occurred in their status within the larger society. Lyndon Johnson acknowledged this in his speech at Howard University in June 1965, one of the greatest speeches on race relations ever delivered. Johnson insisted that freedom was not sufficient. Our goal, he proclaimed, must be not just equality as a right and a theory, but equality as a fact and equality as a result. In his comments Johnson observed that the great majority of blacks remained poor, unemployed, and dispossessed, and for them the walls were rising and the gulf was widening. This was the challenge facing the movement and the country as a whole in the mid-1960s, and its resolution would require a very difficult transformation of mind, thought, and action, particularly for white Americans. Blacks had very little choice but to press ahead. As long as they persisted in their militant posture, white America would be forced to choose between integrity and hypocrisy.

The movement changed the way blacks saw themselves; this was the black revolution. The heightened expectations generated by the civil rights movement and the bitterness fueled by the deep-rooted racial discrimination that thwarted black lives throughout the nation would define the future course of the black struggle for equality. I believed that the NAACP had to be responsive to this militant spirit.

As general counsel, I was undoubtedly the most radical of the NAACP's national leadership. Although I was not a zealot or a nationalist, it did not seem to me that black people could look to white people to help free them from the burdens of discrimination. They had to rely on their own resources to accomplish that objective. My staff and I were on a mission seeking freedom and equality for black people in fact.

By 1965 the staff of the general counsel's office had grown to four lawyers. They were a diverse group. Joan Franklin was a nationalist and talked of blacks organizing their own nation somewhere in the country. Joan was a graduate of Wayne State Law School and a member of the Michigan bar. She was a very good lawyer, and her radical ideas never intruded on the tasks I assigned to her. Barbara Morris, an experienced criminal lawyer, was clearly a member of the black bourgeoisie. Lewis Steel, a young white attorney who joined the staff fresh out of law school, came from wealth. Maria Marcus's family had fled Austria to escape Hitler's Nazi regime.

Our office worked on an agenda consistent with NAACP goals but independent from the national office. We decided what we would do, what cases we would take. In addition to our program to eliminate de facto segregation in education, we were particularly concerned with housing and employment discrimination. We wanted our branches to gain skills in community activity and rely less on litigation. We urged branches to expand their labor programs to take full advantage of the new remedial legislation (Title VII), and to encourage the filing of complaints on the part of aggrieved persons. In all cases, branch officials were urged to coordinate these efforts with the general counsel's office to ensure that the most appropriate method was utilized. Likewise, in the area of housing, we worked with our branches to develop an aggressive housing program that employed new legal remedies provided by federal agencies to challenge the prolonged existence of segregated housing. Federal urban-renewal programs had a severe impact on black communities. We called upon our branches to ensure full community participation in urban-renewal programs prior to federal subsidization and acceptance of those programs.

Roy Wilkins never interfered, but he viewed our office with suspicion, and the tensions were never far from the surface. He was not at ease with people like Joan Franklin. Her views were totally alien to him. He knew I thought her nationalist views were off the wall, and he could not understand how I could have her on my staff. The mind of this once fierce fighter for black rights had become wedded to a belief that the NAACP's survival required it to ally itself to the fortunes and policies of liberal Democratic candidates for national office. This was where the NAACP was situated on the political landscape, although it officially mouthed a nonpartisan policy. I opposed this alliance with the Democrats, not only of the NAACP but of blacks in general. It seemed to me then and still does

now that a fixed political alliance is not in our best interest. We give up whatever clout we might wield, and the
Democrats take us for granted, and then propose policies
adverse to us to lure white voters. Unfortunately, the Republican Party is so filled with conservatives who foster
programs hostile to black interests that it offers no alternative on the national level.

There were many currents of black protest vying for
dominance, and I felt the organization had to try to understand the ideas and concepts being absorbed by the
black community. Black power advocates were having
their moment. Young people were tired of waiting for the
burdens of race to be eased through the law. They wanted
to hasten the process through direct action and mass
protest, publicizing racial disparities. Blacks were talking
with their bodies. I was absorbing all of this. I was learning. These currents were expanding my mind, my vision.
None of this frightened me. The ability to look on even
outrageous acts and concepts calmly and to exhibit respect for the views of the people involved probably came
in part from my being a lawyer. I became attached to
some of the people involved as well. We were the only
group in the NAACP that was conversant with various
political and cultural developments driving black activism
in the late 1960s.

My close friends in the organization had formed a
group called the Young Turks. Dr. Eugene Reed, a dentist
from Amityville, New York, and a leader of the New York
State Conference of Branches, was one of the leading figures of this faction within the organization. The Young
Turks believed that the NAACP should be on the offen-

sive all the time, as did I. At the annual convention in 1965 they mounted an effort to gain a majority of seats on the executive board and to elect Frank Williams to replace Roy. As NAACP general counsel I refused to distort the rules of the organization's constitution and bylaws to favor Roy's group. Nor did I distort the rules in favor of the Young Turks, whose bid to secure the executive directorship and dominate the board narrowly failed. The vote was counted internally, and there was a widely held sentiment, shared by Reed and others, that the results were skewed in favor of Wilkins and his supporters on the board.

A few days after we returned to New York from the convention, Roy called me into his office and accused me of being disloyal to him, and he asked me to resign. I refused and told him I had done nothing to resign for. He could fire me, of course, if he felt he could establish cause. I had taken no direct action against him or in support of the Young Turks, but I was certainly in mind and spirit disloyal to him and wanted his tired leadership, securely tied to the Democratic Party, replaced by more vigorous leadership that would challenge, not accommodate, the white power structure. I told him that if he did fire me, I would challenge and attempt to refute whatever reasons he gave as justification. Since I had a very positive record and my staff was doing a good job, the prospect of a public confrontation apparently did not appeal to him. That ended his thoughts of firing me. Roy hated confrontation and was always concerned about adverse publicity for the organization.

I continued my efforts to orient the NAACP toward a

fuller engagement with the challenges that followed in the wake of the civil rights victories of 1964 and 1965. As black anger and frustration exploded in violent outbreaks around the country, the pressure to act affirmatively in confronting a range of issues was great. The next phase of the civil rights movement, I argued, must be in the area of proposing and enacting a solution. Through its national program and nationwide infrastructure of branches, the NAACP was uniquely positioned to help blacks develop the tools to tackle discrimination in the areas of housing, employment, and education, and lessen the tragic social dislocation bred by decades of exclusion and discrimination.

In the spring of 1966, I proposed a major conference of social scientists, educators, lawyers, and others to address these issues, and work toward devising community tools for a total attack on these problems. My goal was to enroll the best minds in an overall effort to get movement at the community level to a solution of basic issues that were causing misery, discontent, and disaffection among black people.

This plan was scaled back to a conference organized around the issue of education. Kenneth Clark and I chaired the meeting, entitled "Social Science and the Law: A Program for Resolving the Problems of De Facto School Segregation and Insuring Quality Education," which was held in New York on October 20–21, 1966. Participants with presentation responsibility included June Shagaloff; Thomas Pettigrew, a professor at Harvard University, whose field, I believe, was social psychology; William Thompson, dean of the Education School at Howard University; John Fisher, president of Columbia University's Teachers College; and David Cohen, director of the Race and Education Project of the U.S. Commission on Civil Rights. Background papers were distributed in advance of the meeting.

We advised participants to be prepared to discuss and consider the issues that defined the main purposes of the gathering. There were three primary objectives: to make a comprehensive examination of the major issues and problems in respect to de facto school segregation; to determine what the NAACP's major objectives should be in this area, and establish priorities and direction of this phase of its program for the next three to five years; and to establish a permanent advisory committee of social scientists, lawyers, educators, and others to work with the NAACP in planning and implementing the legal and nonlegal approaches to this problem.

June Shagaloff reported on the NAACP drive to desegregate northern schools, noting that by 1966 it had been extended to almost 150 city and suburban school systems in nineteen northern and western states. At least 79 systems had either completed school desegregation programs since 1962 or taken substantial steps toward this end. With the exception of Sacramento and New Haven, however, they were either middle-size or small public school systems. Not a single big-city or large school system had confronted the problem of segregated schools through comprehensive and consistent planning.

Most school boards and public officials, June concluded, did not believe that segregated education was inferior education. They rationalized the underachieve-

ment of black children as a function of their socioeco-
nomic background and adduced a theory of "cultural deprivation." They denied that schools or public policy were
in any way responsible, and contended there was nothing
they could or should do to try and narrow the gap between black and white achievements. While acknowledging that the primary goal of the conference was to explore
education and administrative means for securing equal
education for black children, June advised that the problem was not lack of administrative know-how, but rather
the "unwillingness and the inability of school officials to
bring about change."

Kenneth Clark reflected on what had happened in the
twelve years since the *Brown* decision. He described his
initial belief that there could be an orderly, good-faith
transition to integrated education as wishful thinking.
Resistance to remedying de facto school segregation in
the North was as intense as southern resistance to school
integration. Black children and parents carried the burden of seeking school desegregation, while white liberal
groups, interested in maintaining the status quo, controlled school boards and school systems. It was clear that
a new strategy was needed, along with a reexamination of
the NAACP's core assertion in *Brown* that racially segregated schools could not be equal.

There was a growing emphasis on separatism among
some blacks, who advocated building up black institutions and retreating from the ideal of integration. Kenneth cautioned that any effort to secure equal resources
and support for predominantly black schools would not
lead to easy victory. School boards and public officials

were as resistant to developing and implementing programs designed to improve the quality and efficiency of education provided for black children in segregated schools as they were to all requests for effective school desegregation plans.

Public schools, controlled by white middle-class parents and teachers, had become instruments for blocking rather than facilitating the upward mobility of blacks and other lower-status groups. This was the heart of the problem. Black parents and organizations, then, had to adopt and plan their strategy in light of the fact that the adversaries in the battle for higher-quality education for Negro children would be at least as numerous and formidable as the adversaries in the battle for nonsegregated schools.

Flexibility was essential as black parents and communities explored ways to secure better educational opportunities for their children. But, Kenneth insisted, it must be clearly understood that the objective of increasing the quality of education for black children was not a substitute or retreat from the fundamental goal of removing the anachronism of racially segregated schools from American life. The objective of excellent education for black and other lower-status children, he insisted, must be inextricably linked with the continuing struggle to desegregate public education.

I agreed with Kenneth's assessment. While integration did not necessarily ensure quality education, the integrated school was the indispensable first step toward providing equal education for black children and the best education for all children. There was a growing consensus among educators that de facto segregation did not afford equal educational opportunity for the black child. The challenge that we continued to face, though, was the development of a legal theory that the courts would uphold, one that gave substance and contour to the meaning of equal education in a constitutional sense. With regard to de facto school segregation, the question remained, Does *Brown* apply? Was the equal protection clause of the Fourteenth Amendment capable of reaching all forms of educational inequality provided for under government auspices?

While several cases had been decided in our favor, the balance of court rulings turned on a narrow reading of intent. That is, courts held that segregated schools were in violation of the law only when overt acts to maintain school segregation could be demonstrated. Such a task was exceedingly formidable. How did one examine the mind of a school board official or a lawmaker? Few officials would admit that their actions were motivated by anything other than a desire to create a more efficient school system. In the few cases where proof was available, the resultant effect on the total problem nationwide would be insignificant.

Furthermore, regardless of the intention of school board officials in the 1960s, the existence of de facto school segregation was the cumulative result of governmental policies affecting black access to housing as well as school zoning and enrollment policies. Most important, the equal protection clause of the Fourteenth Amendment mandates equal educational opportunity for black children whenever and wherever the state undertakes to provide public education. Intent was not the issue; results were.

In considering the future course of our legal effort, I sought advice on how we might refine our approach, taking into consideration the practical difficulties facing the courts. Thus far, our theory had a built-in ambivalence, particularly with regard to remedy. The legal argument was clear. De facto segregation, we contended, was a violation of the Fourteenth Amendment because it produced unequal education. But in considering what constituted an effective remedy, a variety of factors had to be weighed, since each school district represented a different facet of the problem.

Remedies had to be designed to meet the particulars of each community and fashioned to eliminate segregation to the greatest possible extent consistent with sound educational policy. What we sought, then, was an honest effort on the part of school boards to produce unsegregated and open schools to the greatest extent possible; but they would not be expected to disrupt the whole educational system. Such an approach, however, permitted the courts and educators a great amount of leeway. As I noted then, if we could tear down all the schools and start again, we'd be in a different situation.

We established a national panel of social scientists and educators to help with the desegregation effort across the country. The goal was to secure the services of psychologists, educators, social policy experts, and others who would be able to help develop and promote well-conceived plans designed to minimize existing patterns of de facto segregation in a particular community. They would be available to work with local school boards who were receptive to developing an effective desegregation program. Where litigation was ongoing, we sought to make experts available to testify in court and study community patterns to show the court alternatives to the present pattern of segregation.

Ultimately, we were unable to make any significant inroads to reverse the pattern of school segregation in the North. In the course of our efforts, we had taken three cases challenging the constitutionality of northern school segregation to the Supreme Court—from Gary, Indiana, Cincinnati, Ohio, and Kansas City, Kansas. The Court refused to review them. Around 1966 I began amassing evidence for a major assault on school segregation in a case involving the Detroit school system. The Detroit school district encompassed the majority of blacks in the city. It was surrounded by school districts in the suburbs that were virtually all white. We sought on constitutional grounds to enlarge the Detroit school district to include the surrounding white districts as a means of eliminating racial segregation of the Detroit schools. I resigned from the NAACP before I could complete the full preparation of the case for trial. The effort was carried forward by my successor, Nathaniel Jones, who completed the preparation of the case, *Milliken v. Bradley,* and won approval of the U.S. Court of Appeals for a metropolitan school plan. In 1974, however, the Supreme Court overturned this ruling and, in a 5 to 4 decision, held that the surrounding suburbs were not required to help provide a solution to de facto school segregation in the central cities.

By December 1968, when I left the NAACP, a small dent in northern de facto school segregation may have occurred, but that dent no longer exists. In the large urban centers of the North where most blacks now reside, school segregation is a fact of life, and the fight to remedy it has stalled. It no longer seems to be the vital public issue it was in the fifties and sixties.

My view is that two factors hindered our drive to eliminate school segregation in the North. To effectively desegrate in the North, where the law does not require racial separation, one must affirmatively use a race-conscious methodology to fight segregation. This seems to be at war with the color-blind society that is supposedly our ultimate goal. The other factor is the fear of white parents that desegregated schooling not only provides no educational benefit for their children but is for them an educational deficit.

Early in 1967, while Gloria and I were vacationing in Barbados, I received a call from Bill Kunstler and Arthur Kinoy asking me to represent Adam Clayton Powell before a special House committee deliberating over whether to seat Powell, who had been accused of misspending travel funds. I agreed to do it and interrupted my vacation to go to Washington. I argued that the committee should advise the House that it had no power to deny Powell his seat, and that even if the power did exist, it should not be exercised in this instance, since the egregious circumstances warranting its use were not present in this case. Congressman Emanuel Cellers, chair of the committee, was persuaded by my argument, and the committee voted to allow Powell to retain his seat, but did vote to censure and fine him. Two months later the full House voted to exclude him from the Ninetieth Congress. Ultimately the Supreme Court ruled that the House had acted unconstitutionally in excluding Powell.

After the committee's vote, there was a gathering in Powell's office. Lawyers and others involved in the case were there, and all seemed to be like Bill Kunstler, seeking to secure payment for services rendered. When I saw Powell alone at his desk, I approached him and told him that he need not worry about any financial remuneration being sought by me, that the services I performed on his behalf were free. That was my way of slapping him in the face—my revenge for his effectively thwarting my prospective nomination to the federal district court.

It probably did not faze him—my slap in the face was not even a tap to him—but I had my satisfaction. It would have made me feel good if he had thanked me and given me a warm handshake, but he was too self-centered to do that. Powell was deeply self-indulgent, and until election time neared produced little for his constituents. Our white friends could not understand how Gloria and I, whom they considered rational, could support such a self-indulgent, corrupt public figure. From time to time, though, he spoke to the heart of black destitution and voiced fierce opposition to whites' unyielding adherence to white supremacy and black subordination. When Powell voiced those views with oratorical elegance, all was forgiven.

I continued to expand the general counsel's office. In

1967, Richard Bellman, formerly an attorney with the Civil Rights Commission, joined the staff, along with Tom Ashley, Robert Van Lyrup, and Ann Feldman, who worked part-time and as a volunteer. We responded to what was going on in the field, representing black teachers who had been fired as southern schools desegregated as well as black students expelled for protest activities at South Carolina State College, Bethune-Cookman, and other black institutions in the South, and also black students at Columbia involved in the takeover of the administration building there. In the Columbia situation I had to convince the administration not to press charges against a group of black students who had staged a sit-in in the president's office to protest the dearth of blacks on the faculty.

There was a wide variety of cases involving the application and enforcement of the Civil Rights Act, along with continuing efforts around schools and education. We won several landmark cases, including two major labor-related cases in Ohio. *Ethridge v. Rhodes*, which Lewis Steel argued, provided that publicly funded building programs could be stopped if hiring practices were racially discriminatory. *Dobbins v. the International Brotherhood of Electrical Workers*, Richard Bellman's case, barred discrimination in the hiring of blacks and whites in skilled trade unions.

Racial tensions were rife in 1968, a presidential election year. The Kerner Commission, a special presidential commission convened to study the causes of the urban rebellions that had swept through northern cities since the mid-1960s, issued its report in March. This bold look at race relations exposed the structural inequities at the heart of the nation's racial problem, and warned that America had become two societies, one black, one white, separate and unequal. Less than a month later, Martin Luther King Jr. was assassinated, and black anger and despair fueled riots in more than one hundred towns and cities across the nation.

That spring, in the face of antiwar candidate Eugene McCarthy's strong showing in the Democratic primaries, Lyndon Johnson announced that he would not run for reelection. Lewis Steel took leave to work for Eugene McCarthy. McCarthy was too vague and ethereal for me, and he had made no issue of civil rights. My support was with Robert Kennedy, one of the few politicians who I believed was sincerely engaged with the problem of racial inequality and economic injustice. He and John Lindsay were the only two white political figures who were completely relaxed among black people. Nowhere was this more evident than with Robert Kennedy's spontaneous address to a mostly black crowd in Indianapolis on the night that King was gunned down. I was planning to take a leave from my position as general counsel and join the Kennedy campaign when RFK was assassinated in Los Angeles on June 5, 1968. I was not in love with Hubert Humphrey. He was a good man, not an Adlai Stevenson phony, but he was tied to the old-style politics on the black issues, and I did not expect far-reaching innovation from him on the race issue.

That summer the NAACP convention met in Atlantic City. The so-called Young Turks were stronger and better organized than ever before. It was estimated that they controlled one-third of the seats on the sixty-member board, and in 1968 they made a final effort to win a majority. Responding to the heightened racial tensions and despair in America's urban areas, the Young Turks pressed for a reorientation of the NAACP's program in light of this urgent situation. They advocated a more community-oriented approach as opposed to a continued emphasis on litigation and federal legislation, and reliance on white-controlled institutions. Their platform called for a greater role for local branches in shaping the NAACP's national programs and policies, and a more concentrated effort on the part of the NAACP to build and strengthen black economic and political power.

These simmering tensions came to a head that fall, around an article Lewis Steel published in the *New York Times* Sunday magazine. The essay, which I had reviewed and discussed with Lewis, offered a powerful and clear-eyed critique of the Supreme Court's record on civil rights. It echoed sentiments that I had expressed, most recently in essays published earlier that year in the *Michigan Law Review* and the *Journal of Negro Education*. In a wide-ranging discussion of the Warren Court in the years following the *Brown* decision, Lewis contended that the Court had struck down the symbols of racism while condoning or overlooking the ingrained practices that had meant the survival of white supremacy.

As was evident in the 1955 ruling on remedy, advising that southern schools desegregate "with all deliberate speed," the Court acted on the premise that racial equality should be subordinated or at least balanced against white America's fear of rapid change. As Lewis noted, some fourteen years after the *Brown* ruling, in May 1968 the Court held in *Green v. New Kent County*, a case involving a highly segregated rural school district in Virginia, that discrimination had to be eliminated from school systems immediately. But there was no indication that the Court was prepared to apply this ruling to the question of de facto school segregation in urban areas outside of the South.

I thought it was a terrific piece. I took a copy of it to Henry Lee Moon, the NAACP's director of public relations. We agreed that the publication of a major article in the *New York Times* by a member of our staff could be used to help with fund-raising. Henry immediately had a huge stack of copies printed, probably fifty thousand. The article appeared on Sunday, October 13, 1968. The editors at the *Times* magazine gave it a provocative title, "Nine Men in Black Who Think White." Lewis later learned that Thurgood, who had joined the Court in 1967, hit the ceiling when he saw the title.

That Monday I met Lewis and Dick Bellman for lunch at a Chinese restaurant and we celebrated Lewis's publication. Coincidentally, members of the NAACP board were meeting in New York that day at the Hilton Hotel. It was not the full board; only around twenty-five members were in attendance. I wandered over to the meeting, and was greeted by the news that at its morning session the board had fired Lewis. The board had just broken for lunch; I demanded of the chair, Bishop Stephen Spottswood, that when it reconvened after lunch, Lewis's firing be the first item on the agenda. When the board convened, I was given the floor to inquire about their firing of Lewis without my being notified. Some members defended their action, saying that the article had not been cleared with the NAACP administration before publication. I said that it had been cleared with me, and that Lewis worked on my staff.

Moreover, I told them I knew of no requirement that articles written by NAACP employees be read and approved by any NAACP official before being submitted to an outside source for publication. I had written articles that were never cleared by anyone, and my pieces had been, I told them, as critical of the Court as Lewis's article. It was not fair to confront the man with an after-the-fact rule and fire him for lack of compliance.

The reality was that their drastic action in response to Lewis's article was aimed at me. It was an effort to exert control over the general counsel's office and bring me in line. Indeed, Roy indirectly confirmed this belief. He was in Paris when the scene played out in the board meeting in New York, but after his return home, he commented to the press that the legal staff constituted "an almost completely indifferent and even hostile segment of the national staff."

Bishop Stephen Spottswood charged that the article was "an indefensible rejection of much of the association's major efforts over the past sixty years," a ridiculous charge. Indeed, the whole basis of the NAACP's contribution to the struggle of the black community for equal citizenship, as I said then, had come only because its lawyers refused to be bound by traditional thinking and traditional concepts. The purpose of the NAACP's legal effort was to break new ground and to develop new concepts of law that could be used in the struggle for freedom. When it denied the right of its lawyers to challenge the contribution of any American institution to the fight against racial discrimination, I warned, it opted for mediocrity and the status quo. Our aim had always been to fight the status quo, not to join it, I argued.

The article aside, the board's treatment of Lewis was arbitrary and irresponsible. He was ousted without even a hearing. Furthermore, the firing of a member of my staff without even consulting me was, as I charged then, personally offensive and demeaning. Protests poured in. The faculty of Howard Law School charged that the board's action was inconsistent with fundamental fairness. The ACLU called the board's dismissal of Lewis "a deplorable act which shocks the American Civil Liberties Union." I announced that I would resign if the board's firing of Lewis were not rescinded. My entire staff were also prepared to tender their resignations unless Lewis was kept on. The board, with twelve members dissenting, refused to reverse its action. My resignation and that of the entire general counsel's office was effective December 1, 1968.

*Chapter 8*

# On the Bench

In the 1960s, opportunities for a middle-aged black law-yer whose professional work had been devoted largely to black causes were limited. White lawyers unfamiliar with the breadth of civil rights jurisprudence believed that civil rights law embraced a very narrow enclosure and that a lawyer who had toiled largely in that arena would be un-able to make a meaningful contribution elsewhere. The reality was that in seeking the legal elimination of dis-crimination one had to become conversant with securi-ties, industrial, business, and other legal issues outside of the civil rights arena. After dealing with the issue at hand you might never need to revisit that particular matter again, but that was the nature of the task of an NAACP lawyer during my tenure with the organization.

The clientele we served were faced with so many var-ied problems that our trays were always heavily loaded with a vast variety of dishes. Yet I had been dealing with these issues for over twenty years—a professional lifetime. I believed my creative energy on this job had been exhausted and I needed another source to recharge my batteries. I was primed to move on, but where? I had not made any plans or investigated the availability of job opportunities, but I feared that my chances of finding a position in which I could stretch my reach beyond present limitations were very slim indeed.

When the story of my NAACP resignation broke in the media in November 1968, with the headline focus being that the firing of Lewis Steel, a white member of my staff, had caused me, a black, to quit the organization, Frank Williams was the first to call to ascertain whether the newspaper reports were correct. On being assured they were, he told me I had a job for a year at the Urban Center at Columbia University immediately on the effective date of my resignation, at the same salary I was now receiving. That lifted a heavy load off me. I think Frank was somewhat disappointed because during my year at the Urban Center I did not begin work on my memoirs or a book on my NAACP career. I was not ready for that at the time and only started work on that task in 2002, some thirty-four years later. Frank was a dear friend and lifesaving benefactor, and I loved him dearly. I regret causing him disappointment.

The year at the Urban Center at Columbia University courtesy of Frank Williams was a godsend. My mind was filled on an almost daily basis with new and diverse ideas. The environment was pleasant and stimulating, and I had a personal revitalization free from the dark menace of

Roy's chronic unrelenting disapproval and was able to engage in intellectual intercourse on a variety of ideas and topics with co-workers. I had a new life.

I wrote several articles and gave several lectures—one of which was a major funded annual lecture at the University of California at Los Angeles—on the persistence of virulent race prejudice and discrimination and the harm to the nation that was thereby being caused. I stayed at Jewel and Derrick Bell's home in Los Angeles when I gave the lecture. Derrick had to be in New York on some assignment during the time the lecture mandated my presence in Los Angeles. Gloria and I planned to spend a week or so with the Bells in Los Angeles, preceded by a weekend for the four of us in San Francisco. Gloria and Derrick flew to San Francisco from New York, and Jewel and I joined them from Los Angeles. We had a great time. San Francisco is such a beautiful and unstressful city that it is difficult not to fall in love with the place. Even one as devoted to New York as my wife admitted that she could be as contented with its environment as she was with New York's. She fell in love with the city and said she could see herself living there, which was quite a concession since before this she had felt she would wilt and fade away residing outside of Manhattan.

After our fun weekend we spent about a week with the Bells in Los Angeles. We were there when Derek Bok called offering Derrick a position as the first black faculty member of Harvard University Law School. Jewel and I were excited. Derrick said he had to think it over. Jewel and I asked: What's to think over? Gloria would not let us pressure him. She made us leave him alone and allow him room and time to consider the offer to his own satisfaction and decide what to do.

Derrick and I have remained close friends. We have shared grievous sadness and joy. Gloria died in 1971 on Thanksgiving Day; Jewel died about ten years later. Derrick remarried. Janet, his second wife, is a lovely woman. She is a professional and her job takes her to California from time to time. She is independent but very supportive of him and excellent with the children, who, after getting over the fact that she is not Jewel but a person they can like and to whom they talk about their problems, have bonded with her. Most of all, she seems to be just the type of person Derrick needs at this stage of his life and career. Derrick has made quite a name for himself as a scholar and writer and is fortunate to have someone like Janet to help anchor his life.

After the publicity about my resignation, I began to be asked to interview for positions at a number of law schools. I was amazed and amused to be asked by people at the University of Michigan Law School to provide transcripts of my college and law school grades. I had been out of law school since 1941 and it was now 1968–69. Since that time I had served in the Army Air Corps and thereafter had a twenty-four-year career in the NAACP trying cases all over country, chiefly in federal courts, and arguing appeals in the U.S. Supreme Court, many of the federal appellate courts, and a few state courts in all parts of the country. I would have thought that it was my experience as a practicing attorney a prospective employer would want to evaluate before making me a job offer. I wondered what was to be gained from my grades. Perhaps they wanted to know what schools I had attended but did not want to ask.

Of all the schools expressing interest in my joining the faculty, I felt most comfortable with Ohio State. It seemed to be a perfect fit. I warmed to the faculty and would have seriously considered taking its offer if I had decided to teach. The downside was that it was in Columbus, Ohio; but I received no offers from any college, law school, or university in New York City. Thus, the possibility of teaching full-time meant relocating outside of New York.

Gloria would not welcome my accepting a teaching position that required leaving New York. In fact, I had become so wedded to the city that the prospect of relocating elsewhere did not sit well with me, either. Then my lucky charm kicked in, and I began to receive partnership offers from a number of law firms in Manhattan. The recruiters from the interested law firms claimed my bringing in clients was not important; they desired me solely for my legal talents. However, I later learned they all felt I would attract paying clients.

All the firms offered an income I had never expected to earn. John Steel, Lewis's brother, advised on what to insist on as a partner in terms of finances and prerogatives. He warned that some so-called partners did not have that status, but were in fact working for and under one of the real partners. Since every offer I received promised income far in excess of what I had ever expected to earn, I could choose the firm where I thought I would most enjoy working. I decided to join Poletti, Freidin, Prashker, Feldman & Gartner in 1969. The income I could expect

to earn there was far less than promised at other institutions, but at this point money was not the deciding factor.
My old friends Herbert Prashker and Justin Feldman
were the reigning partners in the firm, so I felt that I
would be moving into an environment sympathetic to my
need to adjust to a new kind of law practice.

My first assignment on joining Poletti, Freidin was to
represent Trans World Airlines, and in my first month
representing the airline, I billed it for more than the highest income I had heretofore earned in a year. This was a
real eye-opener for me. The firm of about thirty lawyers
(roughly fifteen partners and fifteen associates) was small
even by 1969 standards, but it was a multimillion-dollar
operation nonetheless. I was assured an annual income in
excess of $100,000 as a midlevel partner, and the domi-
nant partners Herb Prashker and Justin Feldman made
considerably more.

I had become close to one of David Rockefeller's assistants, and I brought to the firm a matter from his boss that
certainly impressed my colleagues. I gained a great deal of
status with that account, but I never felt confident that I
could keep bringing in paying clients over the long haul.
(I never had the need to find out, since my tenure as a
partner in a New York commercial law firm was so short.)

When I was with the firm, what most amused me was
how throughout the country, including New York City,
some judges (almost all of whom then were white men)
found it difficult to discern my proper role, since I would
usually be representing a medium- to big-size corporate
defendant. These men could not absorb that a black
would be in that position. For example, one time I was

representing a corporation being sued by a disgruntled employee in the federal district court in Las Vegas. The judge called us to the bench to schedule the date for the forthcoming trial. There were a number of parties involved in the litigation, so a small crowd gathered in front of the bench; mine was the only black face in the group. Each of us told the judge who he was and the litigant he was representing. Since the judge expected a white lawyer to speak for the defendant corporation, my announcement that I was there for that litigant did not register with him at first, and he kept impatiently asking who represented my client. When it finally became clear that the black man standing before them was the corporation's lawyer, he evidenced shock and surprise. To counteract his initial reaction, which had been stereotypical and paternalistic, he next treated those in the courtroom to a monologue about what a great democracy this country was, where equal opportunity was available to all who worked diligently for it, no matter their race, color, or station in life.

My having a partnership in a mainstream small law firm proved very little about equal opportunity in the country or the nature of race relations. What it did show was that for the fifteen white lawyers who were my partners, race was not a delimiting factor in their choice of with whom they would practice law. I am certain that most of what this judge saw of blacks were defendants charged with crime, usually involving illegal drugs, or a black maid or handyman who performed household chores for him and his wife. I doubt that he had ever related to a black person as an equal, and because of the veil separating the black from the white world, he did not know and may have had no interest in knowing that there were a number of middle-class and professional-class black men and women. Although I may not have been the first black lawyer to appear before him, I was apparently the first representing a white corporation, which gave me a status he found surprising that a black man had attained.

His is the commonplace attitude of most whites who tend to think of blacks in terms of the stereotype, even many who have worked and are working alongside many blacks who do not fit that conception. It is difficult for so many whites to reorder their thinking and vision to see blacks as real human beings just like themselves, members of their family, and their white friends. Even white men and women who maintain a genuine friendship with a black do not escape this malady. They too often tend either to forget the race of the friend while keeping the veil of separation in place for blacks in general or to regard the friend as an exception requiring no change in their negative attitude or perception of blacks they don't know.

At first I reported incidents of judges having difficulty seeing me representing one of our corporate clients to my partners, usually Herbert or Justin, expecting them to get some wry amusement, as I had. Far from being amused, they would become upset and angry that I would be subjected to these racist experiences. I stopped sharing such experiences with them. Only in sharing such an incident with a fellow black would I receive the laugh of dry humor I thought was warranted. To a black, my experiences were commonplace, and each who heard my story had been involved in one or more similar incidents. We would end up swapping stories about amusing experiences in dealing with white people.

My partners did not share my fate of potentially being or actually being confronted with some act of prejudice or bias almost daily. They could afford anger, but most of us blacks confront the issue and thereafter for survival deflect the hurt into humor and jest. If I allowed myself the luxury of anger, I would be consumed with an anger all the time that would deprive me of energy to do anything else.

In the summer of 1969, Gloria began to show the first signs of a nerve disorder that would in stages over the next two years weaken, debilitate, and kill her. We were on holiday in the Virgin Islands relaxing on the beach when a bug bit her, causing her leg to swell up to twice its normal size, accompanied by considerable pain. When we returned to New York, it became manifest that something was seriously wrong. She began losing weight and the ability to walk. These factors would worsen in stages. She would decline and remain at a stage of disability for a month or so, and then she would lose more weight and have increased difficulty walking. At each pause, I would hope and pray this would be the limit of her physical deterioration. Her physical disability we could deal with if we must, but she would still be with us. Her being with us was what really mattered. Unhappily, that was not to be.

I took her to every doctor and healing facility that we were told had some expertise or knowledge about the disease that was destroying her. We failed to find a cure, but I now had sufficient funds to provide her with the best care available, including nurses around the clock, and the best physical equipment for maximum comfort under the circumstances.

During all of Thanksgiving Day, 1971, she seemed energized. She had been bedridden for some weeks and could not join us in the dining room for the meal, but I took something to her and she managed to eat a little bit. Our sons, John and David, and several of her closest friends spent time with her and were heartened, as I was, that she seemed energized and in good spirits.

Later that night the boys had gone out to party, and I was in the kitchen cleaning up after the dinner. The nurse told me to go to the bedroom. When I got there and sat by the bed, holding Gloria's hand in mine, she said, "What's happening to me, Bob?"—her last words. A few minutes later her spirit had flown away and her lifeless body was all that was left.

Her death that day was a shock. She had been ill for quite some time and steadily wasting away but never seemingly near termination. David had gone out late to party believing his mother might be better, but when he came home, she was gone. John had left somewhat earlier, so the juxtaposition of his mother energized and dead was not as stark as was David's experience. That was a very bleak Thanksgiving for all of us.

I wanted the funeral and burial to take place the next day, but that did not square with the practices of her family or mine, resulting in my being overruled. Gloria was not religious and was not a member of any church. She was in fact antireligion, believing it to be hypocrisy as practiced, with so few church groups involved in social or community betterment issues. About five days after her death funeral services were held in one of the chapels on the premises of the undertaker we had engaged, enabling family and friends to view the body and say their good-byes before the casket was closed for the funeral services. Derrick Bell spoke the eulogy at the funeral, ending with a poem of Langston Hughes: "I had a friend / And now she's gone away / There is nothing more to say."

My mother and both sisters were still alive and came to New York to be with me, and they along with a number of friends in the building (we were living on La Salle Street) took charge, sheltering the boys and me during the ordeal of the rituals of public mourning, the sitting with family and friends of the deceased and survivors, the funeral, burial, and immediate aftermath. Only thereafter is one allowed full-time privacy to grieve. I will never forget how friends rallied around me and the boys to help us get through this dark period.

This was going to be a very sorrowful holiday season for the boys and me, and I thought it best for all of us to be somewhere other than our apartment and New York for the Christmas to New Year period, 1971–72. I had fallen under London's spell, and since the boys had not been there, I decided that the three of us would spend about ten days in London during the holiday season.

We stayed at my favorite hotel, which I understand was also the favorite of the country gentry. We went to the theater every day and ate in London's best restaurants. We saw some Shakespeare, which the boys ate up. At the end of the ten-day visit we flew back to New York, and our good friends and neighbors Rose and Sydney Reiter met us at the airport with suitcases packed with summer clothing. We unpacked and repacked at the airport.

Equipped with summer wear, we then flew to the Virgin Islands for the remainder of the holiday season. We spent the days on the beach and the evenings in the best restaurants, which were not bad. There were gambling and slot machines at the hotel, and the boys spent their evenings playing blackjack and the slot machines. Neither activity gives me a buzz, so my evenings were spent after dinner with John and David in a cocktail lounge—getting a buzz from a vodka martini or two, my favorite drink at the time, and thinking about Gloria and the good life we had had together. I was, I suppose, grieving and healing. We returned to New York on New Year's Day, 1972. Getting away helped the boys deal with their mother's death, and it certainly was of benefit to me.

In June 1972, much to my surprise, I was called by an aide to Senator Jacob Javits who told me that the senator wanted to submit my name to President Richard Nixon for appointment to the federal district court in Manhattan and asked if I was willing. Since I was a longtime member of the Democratic Party and he was a Republican, this was unusual. Senator Javits felt, however, that a senator of the party of the president, as he was, should not seek to have only members of his political party secure judicial posts. He proposed a formula of three nominees from the senator's party and one from the rival group. Thus a Republican senator with a Republican in the White House would sponsor three Republican nominees and one Democrat. When the senator and the president were Democrats, the senator would propose three Democrats and one Republican.

The call from Senator Javits was totally unexpected. When the potential nomination by President Kennedy in 1961 failed to come through, I had given up all expectation of another opportunity. I did not know the senator and have not ceased to wonder how I got that call. The call may have come of my serving along with Frank Williams on a committee appointed by Mayor Lindsay to find the way to end or at least ease tensions between African Americans and Jews. The retired chief judge of the New York Supreme Court's Appellate Division, who I was advised was close to the senator, had been named chairman of that committee. He may have been impressed by both Frank's and my own levelheaded and reasoned approach to the sensitive and emotional issues we were required to analyze. Frank had far more charisma than I and might have been the judge's first choice to recommend to the senator, but Frank had no desire to be a judge.

I was, of course, more than happy to consent, and the nomination was submitted. There were a number of vacancies on the district courts in New York at the time, and the politicians agreed that these vacancies should now be filled. Thus, many of us from the city were nominated, and we all flew to Washington on June 30, 1972, to appear before the Senate Judiciary Committee, which was to interview us and advise the Senate to approve or disapprove our appointment. The chairman of the committee, Senator Everett Dirksen of Illinois, asked me whether I could be fair to white litigants, which annoyed me, but I was cool in assuring him I would be fair to white people. One other senator inquired whether I knew any admiralty law. I told him I did not, but assured him that no one could possibly be conversant with all the various areas of the law that I understood a federal district judge would be required to deal with from time to time. Because of this one of the first courses in law school was how to find the controlling case law in areas one needed to explore. I do not remember any other questions of significance being put to me, and the question period was brief.

The question about being fair to whites annoyed me because it was a question put to me by every bar group I appeared before in 1972. I am certain no white candidate is asked whether he can be fair to black litigants. The reality of the race climate in the country is that white jurists routinely and continually discriminate against black litigants. Black defendants receive harsher penalties than whites and are offered fewer positive alternatives than are afforded whites. Yet I suppose that to white politicians, all of whom must know that discrimination is rampant, the question is pertinent, for they are seeking assurance that whites will not be subjected to acts of revenge for discrimination against blacks by a black jurist whose appointment they approved.

After completing our interviews by the Senate Judiciary Committee, we all flew back to New York that evening, and when we landed in New York we were advised that the full Senate had approved the appointments of everyone but me. Senator James Eastland from Mississippi was holding mine up to investigate organizations my now-deceased wife had belonged to. I suppose he was looking at my wife's affiliations because except for my college fraternity, the American Civil Liberties Union, the various bar groups, and a life membership in the NAACP—all white-bread institutions—I had joined no organizations.

At first I was not too unhappy about being held up. Thurgood had been held up and not received Senate approval of his appointment for about a year. Connie Motley's appointment to the federal district court in Manhattan had been stalled in the Senate for about six months. I was not as well known as either of them, but being nominated by a conservative president and then sailing through the Senate without a southern senator showing distaste by stalling the appointment would have meant I was regarded as no threat to the racist elements of the South. However, after about a week the holdup produced in me what I call "judgeitis"—fear that the appointment will not come through, resulting in feverish activity to try to secure the assistance of everyone you can reach to help seal the appointment. Until my nomination was stalled I had taken little action to garner support to push it through the Senate. But I really did want to be a federal judge and, infected with judgeitis, I abandoned my cool and began to call on friends to pressure Nixon and Javits and anyone else of influence to help me secure the judgeship. My friends feared that with the nomination stalled, Javits would exert no pressure to ensure that the appointment became a reality, that by getting the president to submit the nomination to the Senate, he had secured the political gain he sought and would do nothing more to secure my appointment. Fortunately, they misread the cards.

On August 17, 1972, I was at Herb Prashker's summer home in Great Barrington, Massachusetts, when I received a call from Senator Javits's office with the good news that Senator Eastland had allowed my nomination to be voted on and it had been approved. I was a federal judge subject to my taking the oath of office whenever I wished.

I decided to take the oath of office in late September, the day after my return from a three-week sojourn in Brazil. I had heard that Brazil had done a far more equitable job of affording equal citizenship rights to its former slave population of black people than was being done in this country. During the last years at the NAACP, I had become attracted to Robert Kennedy, and when I left the organization, I began taking steps to join his 1968 presidential campaign. Earl Graves of the *Black Enterprise* was of the same mind. We had worked together on some matters of interest to the senator. Graves had just begun publishing the *Black Enterprise* and engaged me to write a series of articles on law and business for the magazine.

When he learned of my appointment and my plan to spend three weeks in Brazil, Earl had a member of his staff work up an itinerary for me, and reserved and paid for hotel space, beginning with São Paulo, continuing on to Rio de Janeiro, and ending in Bahia, the area where most blacks lived. He presented me with first-class airplane tickets for my trip and a substantial sum of money for expenses. It was the most generous and thoughtful gift I have ever received other than those from family.

While the *Black Enterprise* was to develop into a huge

public and financial success as the nation's premier publication of its kind, in 1972 all of that was in Earl's hopes and dreams for the future. I have thanked Earl for his kindness and generosity, but what he did was so exceptionally generous and such a warm gesture that it has become for me unforgettable. The trip to Brazil was his thank-you for writing the articles for his magazine, but however beneficial to him my articles were, they were not equivalent to what he did for me. Moreover, it was a wonderful vacation. I came home on September 27, 1972, and was sworn in the next day, well rested, ready to proceed with my new career as a United States district judge of the Southern District of New York.

A large and diverse group attended my swearing-in ceremony. My family was there—my two sons, John and David; my mother; and Alsadene and Alma, my only living siblings. Derrick and Jewel Bell and their children attended, along with Janet and Justin Feldman and their daughters, Diane and Jane; Herbert Prashker and my other law partners; Edward and Rae Dudley (Dudley, now a New York State Supreme Court judge, and I had worked together at the NAACP, and Rae, his wife, was among New York's premier black social elite); and Earl Graves and his wife, Suki Ports, a Japanese American friend who had been a classmate of my partner Gartner's wife at Smith College. Finally, Mayor Lindsay and his chief deputy attended as well. It was said to have been at the time one of the largest turnouts, and the most diverse group of attendees, for such an event in the court's history. Moreover, the group, in its racial, ethnic, and multicultural diversity, was now the face of the nation.

During the ceremony one's family and friends are seated on the floor of the courtroom in a rounded, open reserved space close to the appointee. Rae Dudley brought Mayor Lindsay over to introduce him to my mother. Not knowing who he was or what he meant to me and being introduced to fifty or more people that day, she made a perfunctory acknowledgment and turned away to continue her interrupted conversation. Rae Dudley was horrified. She felt my mother had more or less insulted the mayor. I am sure he did not feel that way, realizing that my mother was being introduced to so many people that she could not keep track of who was who, and she was then about ninety years old. Although vigorous and hale and hearty in appearance, she was still clearly a woman of some years. When I sought to tease my mother about her perfunctory greeting of the mayor, her reply was "He may be the mayor but my son is the judge." That is the response only a proud mother would make.

Carter Bell, Derrick and Jewel's son, added to the fun stories of the day. When, prior to my taking the oath of office, the clerk read the citation of my appointment by President Nixon, Carter Bell piped up in a loud, disapproving tone of voice: "President Nixon didn't appoint Uncle Bob, did he?" with his mother trying to shush him and all of the adults in hearing distance trying to keep from laughing.

The next day I took on my duties as a judge. My first case involved defendants charged with attempted robbery of a bank. When the defendants were brought in I was somewhat surprised that they were black, and my reaction, not voiced of course, was that we had come up in the world—robbing banks instead of the old nickel-and-dime stuff. They had had the misfortune of trying to hold up a bank frequented by FBI agents. When they told the bank cashier to hand over the cash in her possession, announcing, "This is a holdup," the response by one of the agents was: "Like hell it is." It was a clear-cut case.

When I came on the bench in late September 1972, one of my first major cases was a criminal case. After the trial was concluded and the jury verdict was rendered, the assistant U.S. attorney (AUSA) who had prosecuted the case told me in a frank, revealing, and surprising discussion that at the start of the trial, there was no doubt in his mind that he was going to be in full control and running the proceedings. This, in fact, was why he went so far as to admit to me that he had allowed a member of the NAACP to sit on the jury.

On the voir dire examination that occurs at the start of a jury trial, each side is given the opportunity to question each prospective juror about her professional background and to ask for relevant information about her personal life. Thus, the lawyers learn where the prospect has lived and what she has done; whether she is married, single, or divorced; whether she has children, and how many; and if the children are adults, what they do for a living. The purpose of the exercise is to allow the lawyers to get some inkling of whether the prospect would be sympathetic to his cause, since each lawyer is allowed unlimited challenges for cause—reasons making it inappropriate for the prospect to serve. In addition, each side is given a number of peremptory challenges, meaning a prospective juror can be dismissed with no explanation required.

The NAACP juror and I did not know each other, and I refused to allow a challenge for cause. I told the lawyers that I did not know the woman and had been involved in too many activities and had interacted with too many people before becoming a judge to recuse myself unless the relationship with the prospect had been a professional or a close personal one that had been ongoing within the last five years. The prosecutor could have used one of his peremptory challenges to excuse the woman. He chose to let her stay on because he was sure that he would be in control of the trial. He acknowledged, however, that in the end, I was in control.

One of the problems for me and for any black member of a white institution in this country is to avoid the public perception that you accept the status quo. I do this by continuing to write and speak out against discrimination on and off the bench. Early on I presided over a criminal case in which a white American and an Arab American were before me as joint defendants charged with a scheme to defraud investors into buying some bogus stock. The AUSA proposed a longer incarceration for Dolah, the Arab American, than for Weinberg, the Jewish American. I flew into a rage when the proposal was made to me. I liked the prosecutor. He was a bit arrogant but a competent attorney. I am unable to fault a person for arrogance, since I have so much of it myself. The reason for seeking longer incarceration for Dolah than for Weinberg was that Dolah decided to take the witness stand and testify in his own defense and told some blatant transparent lies. It was disgusting, and I chastised him for lying. His lying under oath was the government's rationale for seeking greater punishment for him than for Weinberg, who elected not to testify.

In a criminal trial a defendant is protected against self-incrimination. He cannot be made to testify, and his failure to do so cannot be used against him. While in many cases a jury may hold the failure to testify against a defendant, there are many cases where a defendant who did not testify is found not guilty. So the protection may be effective. Of course, if he does become a witness in his own defense, his testimony can be used against him, as can all the other evidence adduced at the trial.

The problem with seeking a divergence in punishment between the two men was the public perception that the divergent punishment was grounded in racial and ethnic discrimination—an issue to which the government was not sensitive. I told the government's attorney that in presenting such a proposal to me he evidently did not know who I was, because if he had known anything at all about me he would certainly have realized that as one who had fought discrimination all his life, I was not going to give disparate sentences to two defendants—one white, the other not—when both were guilty of the same crime.

The assistant U.S. attorney seemed surprised and somewhat puzzled at my reaction. He expressed awareness of the racial difference but sought to justify giving the white defendant less time in prison because the Arab American had taken the witness stand and told outlandish lies, which I had chastised him for in open court. I conceded the point but argued that the issue here rested on perceptions, and giving Dolah a more severe punishment than his white co-defendant could and would be perceived as an act of racial or ethnic discrimination, and I was certain he did not want such a perception to take hold. I don't think he knew what to make of me.

In the beginning of my judgeship it did not occur to me to try to make the people I worked with more racially sensitive. They had to be when dealing with me, but that probably lasted only until they left my presence. Of course, I had a great impact on my staff; but black judges such as Constance Motley and I also had an impact on the whole operation—judges, attorneys, and court personnel—in many ways. All the judges and court personnel became more sensitized. There was no revolutionary change. I cannot assert that white supremacy and black subordination were not operative—indeed how could that be when they were a primary force in American life?—but they became muted enough not to intrude unduly on the workplace.

When the United States attorney came to see me to defend her assistant, who apparently had reported my reaction to her, I told her that I had great respect for the office she headed but that she had to have her people become more sensitive. The problem with the office was that young white men from middle-class background and elite schools peopled it. They were all decent lawyers and a few were brilliant prosecutors, but the atmosphere was limited and stilted. Some of the people they had to deal with, work with, and prosecute were from another world, as far as they were concerned. They had no idea who these people were, what made them act or refuse to act. At the time there was very little diversity in the personnel in the Southern District of New York U.S. attorney's office.

There was no apparent attempt to rectify the situation. The excuse was that qualified blacks were so in demand that the office was outbid for them. The fact was that no concerted effort had been made to recruit them. I told her she had to diversify the office personnel—more women and more nonwhite attorneys, particularly black and Latino attorneys, were needed.

In all fairness, the Arab American defendant had perhaps earned a stiffer penalty by taking the witness stand and telling a series of transparent lies. Without the racial or ethnic differentiation among the parties, the stiffer penalty would in all likelihood have been imposed. The public, however, would neither have known nor have understood that the stiffer penalty was imposed because of the lies the defendant told on the witness stand in actual contempt of the court. The public would only see two defendants charged with the same crime and the white man being penalized less severely than the Arab American. Explaining the true facts would require a long, complex statement, while all the other side had to do was say he got off because he was white. My statements were overly dramatic, but I could not understand why an experienced prosecutor could not see that differentiation in sentencing between the two men could give the appearance of bias. In a court of multiracial personnel, attorneys, clients, and litigants, one has to be as concerned with the appearance of fairness as with fairness itself.

In another case that occurred early in my tenure as a judge, a group of investors located in Boston were high on a security and embarked on a campaign through radio and television, and the *Wall Street Journal, Barron's,* and other print media, to induce the public to buy the stock. *Barron's*—a magazine that analyzes the value of stocks and bonds—was in its forthcoming issue downgrading the stock. Lawyers for the Boston group tried a clever maneuver. They sought to enjoin *Barron's* from publishing, on the grounds that bad reports about the stock would inflict irreparable harm on the investing public and the Wall Street community. The case was assigned to me. Rudolph Giuliani, then a young AUSA, represented the analyst and *Barron's*.

Freedom to speak and write and to assemble are among the most basic rights of a democratic society. It is one of the most crucial differences between our society and authoritarian regimes. While there are limits to the reach of these freedoms, they cannot be curbed to prevent interference with the profit-making campaign of a security owner. I ruled that the Boston group was attempting to use the courts to subvert *Barrons*'s exercise of its First Amendment rights, tossed out the litigation, and awarded damages to *Barron's*.

Studies show that white judges treat black criminal defendants more harshly than they treat similarly situated whites and give them fewer breaks than they afford whites. As a black judge you can counter that at times.

In 1975, I presided over the trial of a group of blacks known as the New York Nine.* I remember walking into the courtroom for the first hearing in the case, looking over at the defendants, and feeling that these could be my

---

* The individuals involved included Coltrane Chimurenga, Viola Plummer, Roger Wareham, Robert Taylor, Omowale Clay, Ruth Carter, Colette Pean, Yvette Kelley, and Jose Rios.

children. Indeed, in the course of the trial I learned that
Roger Wareham's family were my neighbors and that he
was a law school classmate of my son John. The assistant
U.S. attorney in charge of the case was Kenneth Roth.
Coltrane Chimurenga was an orator who could excite a
crowd. On the first day of the trial, the courtroom was
filled with his supporters. He had just finished a stirring
speech to thunderous applause right before I came into
the courtroom. I wondered whether I was going to have
trouble with them. I always feel I ought to be able to control a situation without seeking help. Doing so to me
means failure, but I was not sure my luck would hold. I
said calmly that this was a public courtroom, not a political rally; spectators were welcome, but the proceedings
demanded that they be quiet. A court proceeding, I
stressed, could be conducted with fairness to all the participants only if spectators listened in silence. I had no
trouble with unruly spectators throughout the trial.

Chimurenga and company were tried as terrorists. Colette Pean was of Haitian origin. Viola Plummer was a
longtime civil rights activist and had once been very involved with the NAACP, but she had become disillu-
sioned with the organization for being insufficiently
aggressive in fighting the white power structure and had
joined this group. Except for Plummer and her son, the
others in the group were young and highly educated.
Chimerenga had a doctorate from Harvard, Roger Wareham was a lawyer with a degree from Columbia University Law School, Penn had an M.D. degree, Omowale
Clay had a graduate degree from a midwestern university,
and Ruth Carter and Yvette Kelley were graduates of

Rutgers University. Young, black, highly educated, and feeling the country would never take meaningful steps to wipe out racial discrimination and injustice, they began to discuss and plan revolutionary steps to effect a change.

The group had begun meeting at apartments at 1700 Bedford Avenue and 80 Millwood Avenue in Brooklyn. They amassed a supply of firearms, began rigorous training in firearms and physical fitness, and began giving similar training to a group of youngsters, along with educational indoctrination. United States law enforcement officials had placed the group under surveillance, and both the Bedford Avenue and Millwood Avenue apartments were wired. The government heard all the talk of disenchantment with the United States and plans to overthrow the government, became alarmed, and then went in with warrants and subpoenas on October 18, 1984, and arrested them all on charges of being terrorists threatening to overthrow the government.

The first disagreement between the government and me was its desire to keep all the defendants in jail until and throughout the trial. If it could not keep all of them jailed, the government desperately wanted Chimerenga behind bars. Since the purpose of bail was to ensure appearance at trial, I felt unless the government met its burden of showing that these people were a threat to the community or would not show for trial, bail was warranted.

The other issue involved appointment of counsel. People brought to trial in criminal cases who do not have the means to pay for the lawyers who are to defend them are entitled to have counsel provided for them by the government. State and federal courts maintain a panel of lawyers who handle the defense of indigent defendants. In the federal courts, it is called the CJA (Criminal Justice Act) panel. Service operates from the top of the panel to the bottom. That is, an indigent defendant is provided with the top name on the panel, name number two becomes top name, and thus the selection process goes through the list.

It does not always work that way. Courts appoint lawyers as CJA attorneys who are not on the panel or appoint a more experienced CJA attorney to handle a particular case. Before the Chimerenga case was assigned to me, it came before Judge Grubin on a bail hearing. She had appointed counsel not on the CJA panel to represent Chimerenga and his co-defendants. Subsequently Assistant U.S. Attorney Kenneth Roth wanted me to deny these attorneys CJA compensation as of the time he brought the matter to my attention.

I asked the parties to show me what the usual practice was. I realized that the government seeks to have indigent defendants assigned counsel from the CJA panel in part because these lawyers are usually less experienced or less skilled than the prosecutors, and life is far easier for the prosecution than it would be if more experienced attorneys were involved. I told the parties that if the usual practice was to appoint only attorneys on the CJA panel to represent indigents and to receive CJA compensation, I would follow that practice. I was not prepared, however, to initiate the practice. The government could not meet that burden, so I refused to dismiss the lawyers who had been appointed by Judge Grubin. They were equal to the prosecutors in skill and experience, and gave Chimerenga and his co-defendants a first-rate defense.

The trial ran for about twelve weeks. Ultimately, I regarded the defendants not as terrorists, but as well-educated young men and women of color who despaired of the hopes and needs of people of color ever being realized under the country's current political and social organization. To them the solution required drastic action. The difference between us was that I believed that social reform resulting in equal rights, opportunity, and justice for people of color could be achieved through peaceful forms of social protest.

Even today many white governmental officials become frightened by acts of aggressive protest against race-, ethnic-, and color-based discrimination and seek to prohibit it by criminalizing the conduct. Before such conduct can be ruled illegal, some illegal act must be performed. In this case the defendants had not yet crossed the line into illegal territory. Thus, they had the protection of the First Amendment validating peaceful protest.

The jury convicted them of the least serious charges: possession of firearms without a license. I made the prosecutor present solid proof of terrorist acts—not talk of acts but the acts themselves—and I allowed the defense full reign to provide a relevant defense. I was convinced that these defendants were frustrated by racism and the resulting denial of opportunities; that they were no more terrorists than I was; and that the revolutionary rhetoric was a dramatic prod—their attempt to find a solution to the country's failure to live up to its promise of justice and equality. They were fortunate that the prosecutors moved too soon when the talk had not ripened into action.

One of the defendants, Roger Wareham, was a lawyer, and on being convicted of possession of unlicensed firearms faced a period of disbarment. When he sought reinstatement, he asked me to write a letter in support of his application, which I did. He was readmitted and seems to be doing well.

I sentenced the others to three months' community service using their professional skills in some appropriate and productive way devised by probation authorities. They were stung sharply for their indiscretions, but not so deeply as to destroy them or end their careers. After serving their community-service sentences, they resumed their interrupted lives, except for Viola Plummer's son, whose obsession with guns has kept him in the custody of law enforcement and prison officials, as this obsession has led to various state criminal law infractions.

These young people were very fortunate to have me preside over their trial. I viewed them with an empathy a white judge might not have had. I myself have been subjected to racial discrimination, as my two sons have been—I could see them frustrated by being denied appointments they qualified for solely because of their race or color. I could see the reason for the misguided belief that only through force could real change be achieved. The veil of racial separation is so thick that few white judges can see a black defendant as sitting where their son or daughter might be if he or she made a mistake or was influenced by the wrong people.

The New York Nine had been toying with the wrong method to solve the problem of race discrimination, but in my judgment long jail sentences were not appropriate under the circumstances. They came away from their trial labeled as terrorists, but without being destroyed. After serving their sentences they were free to return to their former pursuits and could now see that the road they might have started down, but for the government's intervention, would not achieve what they desired: the elimination of racial discrimination, and equality and justice for all. They had paid their dues and could now devote their attention to pursuing their careers. This is precisely what the six college students did. Roger Wareham stops by chambers from time to time, but he has lost touch with his co-defendants in the case.

In 1996 another interesting case came to trial before me, involving a controversy over the leasing of an apartment in Beekman Hill House, a cooperative apartment building on East Fifty-first Street in Manhattan. The occupants of the building were all white. Simone Demou was a cooperative shareholder and cooperative owner of an apartment that she leased to Gregory and Shannon Broome, a racially mixed couple. Ms. Demou advised them that they had to clear the transaction with the chair of the co-op board, Nicholas Biondi. She assured the couple that this was just routine. She had leased her apartment previously and there had been no problem securing the chair's approval.

Gregory Broome, who was black, was a partner in Skadden, Arps, one of the city's premier law firms. As directed, he called Nicholas Biondi and gave the credentials for himself and his wife (who was also an attorney, I believe), and they were welcomed into the building with enthusiasm by Biondi in the telephone conversation. Shortly thereafter, however, when Gregory Broome showed up and met Biondi in person, problems suddenly cropped up, barring his occupancy. Litigation followed, and the case was assigned to me.

The co-op owner was incensed because she wanted the monetary benefit of the transaction and joined in the litigation with the mixed couple. There was a jury trial. The mixed-race couple was represented by young, eager associates of Skadden, Arps, with one of the seasoned partners of the firm on hand to advise and guide the youngsters. Biondi had a very good lawyer, one who traditionally defends clients in race-discrimination cases.

The Broomes sued under the Fair Housing Act and New York Human Rights Law on claims of racial discrimination and civil rights violations after their application for occupancy of the Demou co-op apartment had been rejected by the Beekman Hill House Board, headed by Biondi. During the action, the Beekman Hill defendants counterclaimed for defamation. Demou had become involved in the litigation when Biondi sued her in state court, alleging that Demou had made injurious falsehoods about him to the Broomes. The jury awarded the Broomes $230,000 in compensatory damages and $410,000 in punitive damages, and awarded Demou $27,065 in compensatory damages and $57,000 in punitive damages. I reduced the compensatory-damage award to Demou to $25,310 based on the extent to which her compensatory damages were offset by sale of the apart-

234 A MATTER OF LAW

ment in question. After the jury verdict for the Broomes and Demou, Beekman Hill defendants moved for judgment as a matter of law. I upheld the jury verdict with the minor adjustment in damages awarded Demou.

I regarded this as a welcome opportunity to write an opinion at variance with those heretofore written awarding damages for denial of housing to blacks on racial grounds. Our research revealed that white judges uniformly awarded minimal damages to blacks who succeeded in proving that they had been subjected to racial discrimination under New York's fair-housing law. This belittled the harm suffered, since housing discrimination ghettoizes urban blacks and frustrates efforts to leave the ghetto. I was determined to write an opinion fully justifying a hefty damages award. Accordingly, I upheld the jury awards, with the Demou exception noted, providing a hefty award in damages to a black victim of housing discrimination. I wrote of the harm blacks suffered from housing discrimination, how it forced them to live in worn-out housing, and in general how their choices and opportunities narrowed and limited their housing world. I challenged the reasoning of the minimal damage award precedents as badly argued and lacking in knowledge of basic facts.

I wanted the case appealed in the hope that my reasoning would be adopted, resulting in a decision rejecting the precedents. That was not to be, however. The parties settled the case. I was not informed of the terms, and they are of little interest to me in any event. It was evident that the settlement involved less money for the Broomes and Demou than the jury verdict had awarded them. The lawyers for the Broomes and Demou, aware of the precedents of low awards to victims of housing discrimination, did not want to risk having the hefty awards that I had approved overturned. Lawyers in commercial law firms are not interested in establishing precedents—their chief interest is getting the best money disposition for their clients. Unfortunately, what survives is case law of low judgments for prevailing victims of housing discrimination.

It was, however, a fun case for me. Biondi took the stand in an effort to explain that his reasons for rejecting the Broomes were not racial. He claimed that Gregory Broome was too arrogant and would not make a good co-op tenant because he would cause friction with other tenants. The Broomes had given the co-op board a list of references. No one on the list was contacted to inquire about the Broomes and their ability to mesh with others.

The Skadden, Arps lawyers ripped Biondi apart when he took the stand. He was not gifted with enough intelligence or poise to explain convincingly that his change of mind about approving the lease for the mixed couple after meeting them and seeing that the husband was black was not racist. I suppose it would have been difficult for anyone to provide a convincing explanation aside from color and race.

In my experience, every black man who acts as if he is as good as any white man is now called arrogant. This is the modern, more civilized term whites use. They used to call such black men "uppity." My remarks to this effect were published in a story about the case in the *New York Times*. I received calls from a number of black male friends to tell me that my remarks mirrored their own experiences, and we would have a good laugh. These incidents exhibit a serious flaw in the country's democratic, equal-opportunity front. Blacks find these situations amusing because they indicate that whites really expect blacks to act according to the stereotype, and to accept the subservient status whites assign to blacks.

A final case bears recounting here. Early in my judgeship, as Title VII of the Civil Rights Act of 1964, barring discrimination in employment, became operative, many employers and unions promoted and supported the use of test qualifications for entry-level jobs in a variety of occupations. Tests had not been required until the discrimination bar had become effective, and the tests used initially were not a measure of the skills required to perform the job in question. They were merely generalized measures of the test taker's IQ and general intelligence—the kind of tests in which blacks in general performed poorly and whites uniformly scored far better than blacks. The institution of the tests was a part of the continuing effort to deny or limit blacks' employment opportunities.

I was asked by members of the Guardians to handle a job discrimination issue for them. The Guardians was a group of black men employed in city uniform jobs—police, fire, and transit. The city was planning to institute general intelligence tests throughout the municipal job market. We began litigation seeking to bar introduction of this test on the grounds that the test did not fairly measure ability to perform the job, as it was supposedly designed to do. As structured, the test was designed to measure the general intelligence of the white middle class and thus discriminated against blacks and other racial minorities. The city was required to provide tests that evaluated one's ability to perform the job on an unbiased basis, so that all groups would be fairly evaluated without racial or color restrictions.

The court of appeals upheld most of the requirements imposed. It held in disagreement that the employment selection procedures need not conform to Equal Employment Opportunity Commission (EEOC) and American Psychological standards. It was hoped that the new selection procedures would not have an adverse impact on minorities, but to comply with Title VII the only prerequisite in designing required job tests were that they meet the minimal requirements of the act.

I had handled many employment discrimination cases during my NAACP tour of duty, and employment discrimination was still a rampant problem when I first joined the court. Consequently, early in my judgeship I presided over a considerable amount of employment discrimination litigation. Whenever tests were used I secured a court mandate requiring the city to provide tests of job skills, rather than general intelligence. Thus the requirement that police officers must be five feet six inches or more in height was struck down as being discriminatory precisely because it had no relationship to the job skills a police officer must possess. The requirement would make the average Puerto Rican, who tended to be short, unable to join the police force. In fact, the height requirement had been put in effect precisely to keep Puerto Ricans off the police force. As unions, contractors, and employers realized that the Title VII bar against employment discrimination had teeth, Title VII litigation no longer dominated my caseload.

While it is not for me to evaluate where on the scale of judicial excellence I fall, I do know that I possess a necessary judicial skill: the ability to control a courtroom and move the case along. After a short time on the bench this ability was recognized and the challenges ceased. Many of the lawyers felt that challenging or confronting me was uncomfortably close to racism, and they did not want to go down that road. In 2002 a lawyer of indifferent skill began to operate as if I did not know what I was doing. He initiated incorrect proceedings. I tried to help him right himself, but he ignored me, getting himself entangled in a sorry mess. Since he was such a crude racist, I decided to let him shoot himself in the foot.

I have been on the bench now for over thirty years and it is rare for me to face any overt racism in the courtroom. I am not by nature collegial and do not know all the new judges. I do make a practice of getting acquainted with the new black judges, and black federal judges have been on the bench in New York City since 1961, so we are no longer a novelty. There are not many blacks and few if any Hispanic judges sitting on the federal bench in Manhattan, but there is mutual respect among all of us and some personal friendships.

My first law clerks were Peggy Davis and Jack Novik. Peggy was a Harvard Law graduate: a brilliant and very attractive woman. She had worked as an assistant at Poletti, Freidin in my final year there and she had done work on one or two of my projects. Peggy was working for the Legal Defense Fund when she came on board with me. Jack, my second law clerk, had his program at NYU Law interrupted while he served in Vietnam. After his discharge, he returned to NYU to complete his law school education. I was impressed with Jack in part because his school record manifested growth and maturation. Before serving in Vietnam, Jack's law school grades were Bs and Cs. When he returned to school after his war service, his grades were mostly As and Bs.

Peggy, Jack, and I made a wonderful team. We soon reduced my calendar to a more manageable 500 cases, down from 750, including most of the dogs and many old ones. We soon discovered that some of the old cases that were still viable even proved interesting. One such case involved litigation between individual teams and the National Basketball Association, and I became the final referee of basketball disputes for a time, deciding, for example, disputes concerning whether the claim of a player by the New York Knicks should prevail over one by the Boston Celtics. That was fun. The downside was that I had to give up season tickets for the Knicks. I must have done a pretty good job of suppressing my ardor for the Knicks so that my rulings exhibited no undue, relevant bias, because when the teams moved the dispute-resolution jurisdiction to New Jersey, they asked the judge who was to succeed me to allow me to continue in my old role. He rejected the idea—but I can now be a Knicks fan again.

Jack, Peggy, and I also forged a strong bond of friendship. In fact, Peggy and Jack became two of my closest friends. For much of our relationship Jack was estranged from his wife and then divorced. As a result, he and I spent a great deal of time in each other's company. Jack died about twenty years ago, just shy of being forty years of age. He had become very close to me, like both a partner and a friend. His death was a devastating loss that I feel to this day. When his illness became terminal, my reaction was that it resulted from his Vietnam service, but he assured me that his doctors had found no such correlation.

I realize that I have voiced the same or similar sentiments about good friends on three occasions earlier, but there is no overuse or trivialization involved. My good friend Frank Williams was my own age and ours was a friendship of equals. Frank Reeves was a big brother who had more extensive knowledge of the elite social world than I, as well as my senior in professional experience and in the academy. He had a sharp eye and a keen mind, and was well aware of the hazards that could derail a career and destroy a vulnerable country bumpkin like I was at the time. Frank sought to protect me from hazards that could harm and even destroy me personally and professionally. John Davis was my mentor, a wise intellectual and friend who helped to open my mind to new ideas and hone it to tough-mindedness. Jack Novik's was a bond forged in my mature years, a new attachment but as deep and solid as the others.

What I learned from all of them—the importance of true friendship, hard-core realism, and the power of a well-honed intellect—has enabled me to carve out a career of substance and worth. They took pride in their contribution to my development, and before passing away each knew that I was beginning to fulfill the promise that he had seen and nurtured.

My father died when I was one year old. My oldest brother died when I was about six years old. I never knew him. I sometimes have pictures in my mind of sitting at a table with a very nervous, tense man called Sonny, my oldest brother. Is my imagination at work, or is my mind recalling a real event? My next brother in line lived until I was about twenty-six, but he lived apart from me. He would visit us from time to time, and was an extremely pleasant person, but he made no attempt to influence my growth. I was the first one in the family to go to college and law school, and he took pride in that.

I was raised and surrounded chiefly by women—my mother and sisters. Frank Reeves, Frank Williams, John Davis, and Jack Novik were my mentors, partners, brothers, close friends. They supplied the male bonding in my life. Each of them played several roles at different times in my development. There were other people of influence, but none were close friends like these men. They are all gone now. John Davis was the last to go. He died in late December 2002.

As I take the measure of my life and experience, it is, at a personal level, a story of struggle and triumph. With the support of family and community, I overcame the limits of racial exclusion, discrimination, and poverty to become a leading civil rights lawyer and ultimately a federal judge. *Brown v. Board* sits at the center of my career and of what has been a lifelong struggle against racial inequities and injustice. My efforts and achievements have been celebrated in recent years with countless awards and honorary degrees, particularly during the fiftieth-anniversary celebration of *Brown v. Board.* The most coveted of these was the NAACP's Spingarn Medal. While this has been very gratifying, for me these have also been occasions for setting our sights on what remains to be done to rid this country of the vestiges of white supremacy.

*Brown* remains a pivotal moment in the struggle for racial justice. It launched the movement that overturned Jim Crow in the South and sparked a revolution in black consciousness and race relations, one that transformed America's social and political landscape and continues to resonate to this day. However, the ultimate failure of the courts and of the society at large to remedy the deep structural inequities that cripple the educational opportunity of black children, North and South, is written in the dismal state of public education. "Separate and unequal schools" continue to circumscribe the opportunities of large numbers of black children and other children of color. The crisis facing public education demands the kind of vision, fortitude, creativity, and unceasing efforts that ultimately dismantled legally mandated segregation a half century ago. The struggle to make equality for all people a fundamental tenet in our society continues; the meaning and dynamic legacy of *Brown* provide the foundation for activists and scholars committed to fulfilling its promise.

# Index